USE OF WRITTEN MATERIALS DURING TESTIMONY

	Past recollection refreshed:
1.	A witness may use any writing (or photograph) for the purpose of refreshing his present recollection.
2.	Witness may not read from writing.
3.	The writing is not entered into evidence.

	Past recollection recorded:
1.	When a witness has insufficient recollection of an event for him to testify accurately and fully (even after having his recollection refreshed), he may read into evidence a writing if the proper foundation is laid.
2.	The witness will read the writing into evidence.

THERE ARE FIVE WAYS TO IMPEACH A WITNESS

	Impeachment type:	Method of introduction:	
1.	Prior Inconsistent Statements	Cross	Extrinsic Evidence
2.	Bias, Interest, Hostility	Cross	Extrinsic Evidence
3.	Conviction of Crime (Felony or Dishonesty)*	Cross	Record of Judgment
4.	Specific Instances of Misconduct (Bad Acts)	Cross	
5.	Opinion/Reputation for Truthfulness	Other witnesses	

* Judgments of felony are admissible in criminal and civil actions to prove any fact essential to the judgment (motive or intent).

CONVICTION OF CRIME (FELONY OR DISHONESTY)—CRIMES

1. Any crime, if the crime was punishable by death or imprisonment in excess of one year, and the probative value of admitting the evidence outweighs its prejudicial effect to the accused. [FRE 609(a)]
2. Any crime regardless of punishment, if proving the crime requires proof or admission of an act of dishonesty or false statement by the witness. [FRE 609(b)]
3. The conviction should not be older than 10 years.
   a. In a criminal case, felonies of witnesses may be used ONLY for impeachment.

OPINION/REPUTATION FOR TRUTHFULNESS

Counsel may NOT ask about arrests (an arrest in and of itself is not a bad act).

HEARSAY

DEFINITON

Hearsay is an out-of-court statement offered for the truth of the matter asserted. [FRE 801] Hearsay is inadmissible in court, because the adverse party has been denied the opportunity to cross-examine the declarant (one who offers the hearsay).

STATEMENT

If a statement is hearsay, an exception must be found in order for the statement to be admitted as evidence. [FRE 802]

NONHEARSAY

Under the Federal Rules of Evidence, the following are NOT considered hearsay. Thus, they are admissible as substantive evidence. [FRE 801(d)].

Note: State-based Rules of Evidence may consider the following as "exceptions" rather than "nonhearsay." The distinction is inconsequential; both categories operate to admit the statement as evidence.

Prior Statement by Witness
[FRE 801(d)(1)]

1. **Prior inconsistent statement:** If the prior statement of a witness, given under oath of a previous proceeding, is inconsistent with the declarant's in-court testimony, then it may not be admitted as nonhearsay. [FRE 801(d)(1)(A)] [*State v. Smith*, 651 P.2d 207 (Wash. 1982)]
2. **Prior consistent statements:** However, if the prior statement (given under oath at a previous proceeding) is consistent with the declarant's in-court testimony and is offered to rebut a charge of bias or improper motive, then the statement may be admitted as nonhearsay. [FRE 801(d)(1)(B)] [*Tome v. United States*, 513 U.S. 150 (1995)]
3. **Prior identification:** A statement identifying a person as someone seen by the witness is admissible as nonhearsay. [FRE 801(d)(C)] [*State v. Motta*, 659 P.2d 745 (Hawaii 1983)]

Admissions by Party Opponent

1. **Admissions:** An admission is a statement made (about a relevant fact) or act that amounts to a prior acknowledgment by one of the parties. The statement need not be against the declarant's interests at the time it was made. Compare with declarations against interest. [FRE 801(d)(2)(A)]
2. **Adoptive admissions:**
   a. A party may make an admission by adopting the statement of another. [FRE 801(d)(2)(B)] [*United States v. Hoosier*, 542 F.2d 687 (1976)]
   b. Silence may be indicative of an adoptive admission only in narrow circumstances.
      i. Only if a party heard and understood the statement;
      ii. The party was capable of denying the statement;
      iii. A reasonable person would have denied the statement.

   Note: It is very important to remember that silence as an adoptive admission NEVER applies in a criminal case.
3. **Vicarious admissions:** Agent/employee statements concerning any matter within the scope of the agency/employment made while the employment relationship exists are admis-

[illegible] principal/employer [FRE

[FRE 801(d)(2)(E)]

RESIDUAL "CATCH-ALL" EXCEPTION
[FRE 807]

1. Hearsay statement must possess circumstantial guarantees of trustworthiness;
2. The statement must be strictly necessary; and
3. Notice must be given to the adversary as to the nature of the hearsay. [*State v. Weaver*, 554 N.W.2d 240 (1996)]

FOUR TYPES OF HEARSAY EXCEPTIONS WHERE THE DECLARANT MUST BE UNAVAILABLE

Former Testimony [FRE 804(B)(1)]

1. Statement made under oath and subject to cross-examination at another proceeding.
2. Former testimony is admissible to the party who offered it in the prior proceeding and had the same motive and opportunity to develop testimony.
3. Former testimony is also admissible by a prior opponent who had the same motive and opportunity to cross-examine the declarant then as now.
4. Grand jury testimony does not suffice as former testimony. If the statement is classified as a prior inconsistent statement under oath (which is nonhearsay), grand jury testimony is admissible both as substantive truth and for impeachment purposes. [*Lloyd v. American Export Lines, Inc.*, 580 F.2d 1179, *cert. denied*, 439 U.S. 969 (1978)]

Dying Declarations [FRE 804(B)(2)]

1. The declarant must be dying or under a sense of immediately impending death.
2. The dying declarant must have personal knowledge of the facts.
3. The statement must concern itself with the facts and circumstances surrounding the supposed death.
4. Dying declarations may only be admitted for homicide charges in a criminal case, while in civil trials, they may be admitted for all purposes within the above limits.

Declarations Against Interest
[FRE 804(B)(3)]

1. Statement must be made against interest (pecuniary or penal) when made (declarant must be aware of such criminal or financial liability when statement is made).
2. Declarant must have personal knowledge of facts.
3. Declarant must be unavailable.
4. Declarant must not be a party. [*Williamson v. United States*, 512 U.S. 594 (1994)]

Declarations About Personal or Family History [FRE 804(B)(4)]

Statements concerning the declarant's own birth, adoption, marriage, divorce, legitimacy, or relation by blood, adoption, marriage, ancestry, or other similar fact.

Hearsay continues on page 4 ▶

PRIVILEGES

DEFINITION

Privileges permit the one who is invoking them to refuse to disclose, and prohibit others from disclosing, certain confidential communications during judicial proceedings.

1. Only the holder of the privilege may assert the privilege.
2. The communication in question must also be confidential.
3. Neither counsel for the parties nor the judge may comment on a claim of privilege.

PRIVILEGE AGAINST SELF-INCRIMINATION

Under the Fifth-Amendment of the Constitution, a witness may not be compelled to testify against herself. The witness may refuse to give an answer that ties the witness to the commission of a crime. [*Griffin v. California*, 380 U.S. 609 (1965)]

WAVIER

Enumerated privileges may be waived by:

a. Failure to assert the privilege; OR
b. Voluntary disclosure of the subject matter by the holder of the privilege.

ATTORNEY-CLIENT PRIVILEGE

Attorney and client communications, made during consultation, are privileged from disclosure.

1. The client must be seeking the professional services of the attorney in order for the privilege to apply.
2. Communication must be confidential in nature (i.e., the client does not wish others outside of those representing the attorney to know of communication). [*People v. Meredith*, 631 P.2d 46 (Cal. 1981)]
3. The attorney-client privilege lasts forever.
4. Client holds the right to assert the attorney-client privilege. The attorney-client privilege will not apply in the following cases:
   a. When the relevant communication in question involves a dispute between attorney and client; OR
   b. If the lawyer's services were sought to aid in the commission of a crime by the client.

MARITIAL PRIVILEGES [FRE 501]

There are two types of privileges that may be invoked between two formerly or currently married people:

- Confidential Marital Communications [*United States v. Montgomery*, 384 F.3d 1050 (2004)]
- Spousal Testimony [*Trammel v. United States*, 445 U.S. 40 (1980)]

The marriage privileges do not apply in actions between the spouses, or against the testifying spouse, or the children.

Confidential marital communications: *(Civil and Criminal)*	**Spousal testimoney:** *(Criminal Only)*
Only applies to communications made during marriage	Applies to communications made before marriage as well as during
Theoretically lasts forever	Divorce destroys
Either spouse may claim privilege	Only witness spouse may claim

PHYSICIAN/PATIENT PRIVILEGES

Federal court does not recognize physician/patient privilege (state law may work). [*Jaffee v. Redmond*, 518 U.S. 1 (1996)]. Be careful of examination made at the request of an attorney—if there is no treatment contemplated, there is no privilege, but the attorney/client privilege will attach.

a. When patient puts physical condition in issue, privilege is waived.
b. Not a privilege, but statements of past physical condition to a doctor employed to testify are admissible under the FRE.

TESTIMONIAL EVIDENCE

OPINION TESTIMONY

1. **Lay witness:** Generally, opinion evidence by a lay witness is inadmissible unless:
   a. The opinion is based on personal knowledge, not on scientific, technical, or other specialized knowledge.
   b. There is "rational basis" for the opinion.
   c. The opinion is helpful to a clear understanding of the testimony or allows a trier of fact to determine the facts. [FRE 701]
2. **Expert witness:** If qualified as an expert in the subject, the witness may give opinion testimony, even without personal knowledge. [FRE 702]
   a. However, the opinion given by the expert witness must be supported by a proper factual basis, which may be provided by one of three ways:
      i. Personal observation;
      ii. Facts made known to the expert before or during trial; [FRE 703]
      iii. Facts supplied to the expert prior to trial and of a type reasonably relied upon by experts in the particular field. [FRE 703] [*Daubert v. Merrell Dow Pharmaceuticals*, 509 U.S. 579 (1993); *Kumho Tire Co., Ltd. v. Carmichael*, 526 U.S. 137 (1998)]
   b. An opponent may use authoritative texts and treatises in the field of expertise to contradict the testimony of the expert. Such treatises are admissible as substantive evidence. [FRE 803(18)]
   c. Ultimate Issue Rule:
      i. In a criminal case in which the defendant's mental state constitutes an element of the crime or defense, an expert witness may NOT state an opinion as to the ultimate issue of the defendant's mental state. [FRE 704(b)]
      ii. In all other cases, an expert witness may render an opinion as to the ultimate issue in a case. [FRE 704(a)]

REHABILITATION

1. If a witness has been attacked on his veracity, witnesses may offer reputation for truthfulness. [FRE 608]
2. A party may not ordinarily rehabilitate a witness by showing a prior consistent statement (even when attacked with a prior inconsistent statement).
   a. However, if witness has been attacked for being biased or recently fabricating testimony, a prior consistent statement may be introduced to rebut the evidence and it will stand for substantive truth.

WITNESS COMPETENCE

A witness is NOT disqualified as incompetent because of personal characteristics that may make his testimony suspect. [FRE 601]

NONRESPONSIVE ANSWERS

If the answer is not responsive to the question asked, then the answer may be stricken from the record.

IMPEACHMENT

Impeachment means casting an adverse reflection on the character or truthfulness of the witness. A witness may be impeached by any party. One may impeach one's own witness. In impeachment, evidence of the credibility of the witness must be produced by some means other than cross-examination of the witness. (*See* "5 Ways to Impeach a Witness" chart.)

LEADING QUESTIONS

1. Leading questions are generally questions that suggest to the witness an answer that an examining party desires.
   Leading questions may not be used during direct examination unless they concern:
   a. Preliminary matters; OR
   b. Witness is hostile (one may call one's own witness as a hostile witness).
   Leading questions are permissible during cross-examinations.

PAST RECOLLECTION RECORDED—[FRE 803(5)] FOUNDATION

1. Witness had personal knowledge of the facts in the writing.
2. The writing was made by the witness (or it was adapted by her).
3. The writing was made when the matter was fresh in the witness's mind.
4. The writing is accurate.
5. The witness is unable to testify fully and accurately due to insufficient recollection. [*Ohio v. Scott*, 285 N.E.2d 344 (Ohio 1972)]

Testimonial Evidence continues on page 3 ▶

QUICK COURSE OUTLINE

EVIDENCE

This outline is based on the Federal Rules of Evidence and does not include local jurisdictions' Rules of Evidence.

RELEVANCE

DEFINITON

All evidence must be relevant. Relevant evidence is evidence that has a tendency to disprove or prove any fact that may affect the outcome of the action. [FRE 401]

The judge in any case has the discretion to exclude relevant evidence if its probative value is substantially outweighed by the danger of unfair prejudice, confusion of the issues, or misleading the jury, or by schedule considerations. [FRE 403]

EVIDENCE THAT MAY BE EXCLUDED FOR POLICY REASONS

1. Liability Insurance: Evidence that a person has liability insurance covering her acts is not admissible to prove that she has performed those acts negligently or wrongfully. [FRE 411]
2. Subsequent Remedial Measures: Evidence that a party took action that might have prevented the incident in litigation is not admissible to prove that the party was negligent or reckless, or that a product was defective. [FRE 407]
3. Settlement Offers: Evidence of a settlement offer (or statements made during settlement negotiations) made at the time the likelihood of the litigation was possible will not be admissible to prove fault. Also, the claim in question must have a dispute as to liability or amount. [FRE 408]
4. Plea Bargains: Evidence that a criminal defendant engaged in plea bargaining with the prosecutor, including statements in negotiations, or that he entered a plea of *nolo contendere* is inadmissible against the defendant. The same applies to withdrawn guilty pleas. [FRE 410]
5. Payment or offers to pay for injured party's medical expenses are inadmissible. [FRE 409]

CHARACTER EVIDENCE

CRIMINAL–CHARACTER EVIDENCE

1. Character evidence is inadmissible if offered by prosecutor to show defendant has a propensity to commit crimes. [FRE 404(a)]
2. Character evidence is admissible if offered by defendant to show character not in keeping with crime charged.
   - **a.** Offered by witness: Reputation and opinion only.
   - **b.** Character evidence is rebutted by plaintiff or prosecution calling witnesses whose testimony is similarly limited (reputation & opinion). [FRE 404(a)(1)] The plaintiff or prosecutor may rebut such character evidence for "good character" because the defendant has "opened the door" to his character.
3. Victim's "bad" character may also be introduced into evidence by defendant [FRE 404(a)(2)] except in rape cases, where Rape Shield Laws apply. [FRE 412]:
   - **a.** Rape victim's past behavior (in civil and criminal cases) is, generally, NOT admissible.
     - **i.** Criminal cases: May use it to prove consent ONLY between defendant and victim.

HABIT

Habit is distinguished from general "character" of witness as repetitive human behavior that is specific, frequent, invariable, and visible.

Character evidence: "Jimmy is a drunk."

Habit evidence: "Jimmy always stops by Betty's for a few drinks every night after work."

Habit evidence is usually admissible to prove that a person acted in conformity with that habit. Habit may be proved by opinion or specific evidence. [FRE 406]

EVIDENCE THAT MAY BE EXCLUDED FOR POLICY REASONS

	Evidence that may be excluded:	But may be admissible:
1.	Liability Insurance [FRE 411]	To prove ownership, impeachment, or as an admission
2.	Subsequent Remedial Measures [FRE 407]	To prove ownership
3.	Settlement Offers [FRE 408]	For everything except to prove liability
4.	Plea Bargain [FRE 410]	Not admissible at all (different from a conviction)
5.	Offers to Pay Medical Expenses [FRE 409]	Admissions of fact that accompany an offer

ADMISSIBILITY OF CHARACTER EVIDENCE

CRIMINAL & CIVIL

1. Reputation or opinion evidence of a person's character for truth and veracity is permissible to impeach her, if she testifies as a witness. If, and only if, she is so impeached, similar kinds of evidence are admissible to rehabilitate her credibility (*see* Impeachment). [FRE 608(a)]
2. Inadmissible if the probative value is substantially outweighed by unfair prejudice. [FRE 403]
3. Evidence of acts similar to defendant's sexual assault and child molestation are admissible in criminal cases [FRE 413, 414], and in civil cases [FRE 415(a)]. In civil cases, proper notice is required [FRE 415(b)].

CIVIL–CHARACTER EVIDENCE

1. Is inadmissible if offered to show that either party acted in conformity with that character trait. [FRE 404(a)]
2. Is admissible if character is an issue:
   - **a.** Defamation, negligent hiring, negligent entrustment, etc.

METHODS OF PROVING CHARACTER EVIDENCE

Once it has been determined that character evidence is admissible, there are three ways in which to introduce such evidence (all three may not always be available):

1. Reputation;
2. Opinion (*see* Opinion Testimony);
3. Specific instances. [FRE 405]

JUDICIAL NOTICE

DEFINITION

Judicial notice establishes a fact as true during a trial. Courts take judicial notice of adjudicative facts if they are indisputable because they are commonly known or may be ascertainable.

PRACTICAL EFFECT

1. Criminal: A judge will instruct the jury that it may, but it is not required to, accept the fact conclusively. [FRE 201]
2. Civil: Creates an irrebuttable presumption (more or less conclusive). Courts must take judicial notice of federal and state law. Municipal ordinances, private acts, legislative resolutions, and foreign laws may be noticed, at the discretion of the court.

UNAVAILABILITY

A declarant is considered "unavailable" if:

- **a.** One of the enumerated privileges triggers unavailability, i.e., prevents the declarant from testifying;
- **b.** Declarant refuses to testify, despite a court order;
- **c.** Declarant is dead;
- **d.** Declarant is unable to testify due to illness;
- **e.** Declarant is beyond the reach of the court's jurisdiction. [FRE 804(a)] [*Barber v. Page*, 390 U.S. 719 (1968)]

"FOR THE TRUTH OF THE MATTER ASSERTED"

If the out-of-court statement is introduced for any purpose other than to prove the truth of the matter asserted, there is no need to cross-examine the declarant. The statement is not hearsay. The following are examples that are not hearsay:

1. Legally operative facts/conduct, e.g., words of a contract, defamatory statements, etc., are not offered for the truth of the matter asserted.
2. Statements offered to show their effect on the hearer or reader.
3. Statement offered as circumstantial evidence of declarant's state of mind.
4. Any use for which the statement is relevant irrespective of its truth or falsity.

HEARSAY EXCEPTIONS (UNAVAILABILITY IMMATERIAL)

1. **Present sense impressions:** A statement made concurrently or immediately thereater with perception of event described. [FRE 803(1)] [*Nuttall v. Reading Co.*, 235 F.2d 546 (1956)]
2. **Excited utterance:** Statement made under the stress of excitement from a startling event that the declarant was perceiving. [FRE 803(2)]
3. **State of mind or "present state of mind":** Declaration of then-existing state of mind, emotion, sensation, or physical condition. This is usually used to establish intent. [FRE 803(3)] [*United States v. Pheaster*, 544 F.2d 353 (1976), *cert. denied*, 429 U.S. 1099 (1979)]
4. **Statements of medical diagnosis:** Statement made to medical personnel for the purpose of diagnosis and treatment, such as the medical history or cause of condition. [FRE 803(4)]
5. **Past recollection recorded:** Writing by witness who cannot now remember the facts. Written while the events were still fresh in her mind. [FRE 803(5)] *See* "Past Recollection Recorded" under "Testimonial Evidence."
6. **Business records:** Writing made during the regular course of business by someone with personal knowledge and a business duty to transmit the records. Records made for the purposes of litigation do NOT qualify. Also, lack of such a business record may be used to show a nonoccurrence of an event. [FRE 803(6)]
   Note: Police reports do not qualify under the business records exception to hearsay. However, police reports may qualify as a public record.
7. **Official records/public records**: Records from public agencies concerning their activities (such as births, deaths, marriages, and official acts of the public agency). Lack of such writing may be admissible to indicate a nonexistence of the matter. [FRE 803(8)]
   - **a.** Criminal purposes:
     - **i.** Prior felony convictions are admissible in both civil and criminal surroundings.
     - **ii.** In a criminal case, the government may use the prior felony conviction only against the accused. Against all others it must be used for impeachment purposes.
     - **iii.** Prior civil judgments may be admitted in criminal trials. Note that a prior civil judgment will NOT be admissible for subsequent civil trials.
     - **iv.** The matters observed by a police officer in a police report are inadmissible.

   Note: Public records and reports (i.e., factual findings of a government agency) are usually NOT admissible against the defendant in a criminal case. (Police reports are not business records, although they may be partially admitted in a civil case under public records—they may be used against the government in a criminal case.)

CONFESSIONS

1. A confession must be taken outside the presence of the jury; in all other matters, judge has a great deal of discretion.
2. Statements made in violation of the Miranda rule are admissible at trial, under the exclusionary rule, but the confession may be used for impeachment purposes.

FINDING HEARSAY OBJECTION

What is considered a statement:

- **a.** A statement, for purposes of the hearsay rule, can be an oral or written assertion.
- **b.** A non-verbal conduct intended as an assertion (e.g., pointing of the finger) may also be a statement for hearsay purposes. [FRE 801(a)(2)]
- **c.** Nonhumans may not transmit hearsay.

WRITTEN EVIDENCE

AUTHENTICATION

"Authentication" means proving that a writing or object is what the proponent of the evidence claims. It is required before documentary evidence may be admitted. [FRE 901(a)]

DOCUMENTS

A writing may be authenticated by:

1. Direct Testimony: Testimony of one who sees it executed or hears it acknowledged. [FRE 901(b)(1)]
2. Handwriting Verification: The opinion of a non-expert with personal knowledge of the writer's handwriting. [FRE 901(b)(2)] This sort of authentication may also be done by a trier of fact through comparison of the disputed writing with an exemplar proven to be of the original writer. [FRE 901(b)(3)]
3. Distinctive Characteristics: Evidence related to appearance, contents, substance, internal patterns, or other characteristics in context. [FRE 901(b)(4)] [*United States v. Bagaric*, 706 F.2d 42 (1983)]
4. Ancient Documents: Evidence that is at least 20 years old and it was found in a likely place. The document must also be free of any suspicion as to its authenticity. [FRE 901(b)(8)]
5. Computers/Machines: A document produced by some mechanical or electronic process may be authenticated if it is shown that the process operated accurately. [FRE 901(b)(8)]
6. Admission: Evidence that the party against whom it is offered has either admitted its authenticity or acted upon it as authentic.
7. Photographs: Admissible only if identified by a witness as a portrayal of facts relevant to the issue and verified by such a witness as a correct representation of those facts. The original photographer need not testify.
8. Self-Authenticating Documents: [FRE 902] Examples of documents that need no extrinsic evidence of authenticity: certified copies of public records; official publications; newspapers and periodicals; trade logos and inscriptions; and commercial paper (UCC).

BEST EVIDENCE RULE ("ORIGINAL DOCUMENT RULE")

To prove the terms of a writing (if the terms of the writing are material), the original writing must be produced. Secondary evidence (testimony or copies) is admissible only if the original is unavailable.

1. The Best Evidence Rule usually applies in situations where the writing is a legally operative or dispositive instrument.
2. The rule only applies when the proponent is trying to prove the content of the writing. It does not apply when the proponent is attempting to prove that something that happened is simply recorded in that writing.
3. An "original" is the writing itself or any duplicate that is intended by the person executing it to have the same effect.
   - **a.** A duplicate is an exact copy of an original (e.g., photocopies or certified public copies).
   - **b.** Duplicates are admissible as long as there is no dispute about the authenticity of the original or other unfairness in the use of the duplicate. [FRE 1003]
4. Secondary evidence of the contents (copies, notes, oral testimony) of an "original" writing may be given if the following apply:
   - **a.** Loss or destruction of the original; [FRE 1004(1)]
   - **b.** Original document is unavailable; [FRE 1004(1)]
   - **c.** Adversary possesses the original document. [FRE 1004(3)]

ORAL STATEMENTS

1. Voice Identification: A voice may be identified by the opinion of anyone who has heard the voice at any time. A witness may also hear the voice after litigation has begun for the sole purpose of testifying. [FRE 901(b)(5)]
2. Telephone conversations: A speaker engaged in a telephone conversation may be authenticated by the other party to the conversation through various means:
   - **a.** if a witness dials the number listed for the person and the person who answers the phone identifies herself as that person; [FRE 901(b)(6)]
   - **b.** if a witness dials a business and talks with the person answering the phone about matters relevant to the business;
   - **c.** if a witness testifies that the speaker had knowledge of certain facts that only a particular person would have;
   - **d.** and, of course, if the witness recognizes the other speaker's voice.

CASENOTE® Legal Briefs®

EVIDENCE

Keyed to Courses Using

Mueller, Kirkpatrick, and Richter's Evidence Under the Rules: Texts, Cases, and Problems Tenth Edition

Authored by: Publisher's Editorial Staff

ASPEN PUBLISHING

To contact Customer Service, e-mail customer.service@aspenpublishing.com, call 1-800-950-5259, or mail correspondence to:

Aspen Publishing
Attn: Order Department
1 Wall Street
Burlington, MA 01803

Printed in the United States of America.

1 2 3 4 5 6 7 8 9 0

ISBN 978-1-5438-5083-3

About Aspen Publishing

Aspen Publishing is a leading provider of educational content and digital learning solutions to law schools in the U.S. and around the world. Aspen provides best-in-class solutions for legal education through authoritative textbooks, written by renowned authors, and breakthrough products such as Connected eBooks, Connected Quizzing, and PracticePerfect.

The Aspen Casebook Series (famously known among law faculty and students as the "red and black" casebooks) encompasses hundreds of highly regarded textbooks in more than eighty disciplines, from large enrollment courses such as Torts and Contracts to emerging electives such as Sustainability and the Law of Policing. Study aids such as the *Examples & Explanations* and the *Emanuel Law Outlines* series, both highly popular collections, help law students master complex subject matter.

Major products, programs, and initiatives include:

- **Connected eBooks** are enhanced digital textbooks and study aids that come with a suite of online content and learning tools designed to maximize student success. Designed in collaboration with hundreds of faculty and students, the Connected eBook is a significant leap forward in the legal education learning tools available to students.
- **Connected Quizzing** is an easy-to-use formative assessment tool that tests law students' understanding and provides timely feedback to improve learning outcomes. Delivered through CasebookConnect.com, the learning platform already used by students to access their Aspen casebooks, Connected Quizzing is simple to implement and integrates seamlessly with law school course curricula.
- **PracticePerfect** is a visually engaging, interactive study aid to explain commonly encountered legal doctrines through easy-to-understand animated videos, illustrative examples, and numerous practice questions. Developed by a team of experts, PracticePerfect is the ideal study companion for today's law students.
- The **Aspen Learning Library** enables law schools to provide their students with access to the most popular study aids on the market across all of their courses. Available through an annual subscription, the online library consists of study aids in e-book, audio, and video formats with full text search, note-taking, and highlighting capabilities.
- Aspen's **Digital Bookshelf** is an institutional-level online education bookshelf, consolidating everything students and professors need to ensure success. This program ensures that every student has access to affordable course materials from day one.
- **Leading Edge** is a community centered on thinking differently about legal education and putting those thoughts into actionable strategies. At the core of the program is the Leading Edge Conference, an annual gathering of legal education thought leaders looking to pool ideas and identify promising directions of exploration.

Format for the Casenote® Legal Brief

Nature of Case: This section identifies the form of action (e.g., breach of contract, negligence, battery), the type of proceeding (e.g., demurrer, appeal from trial court's jury instructions) or the relief sought (e.g., damages, injunction, criminal sanctions).

Party ID: Quick identification of the relationship between the parties.

Fact Summary: This is included to refresh your memory and can be used as a quick reminder of the facts.

Rule of Law: Summarizes the general principle of law that the case illustrates. It may be used for instant recall of the court's holding and for classroom discussion or home review.

Facts: This section contains all relevant facts of the case, including the contentions of the parties and the lower court holdings. It is written in a logical order to give you a clear understanding of the case. The plaintiff and defendant are identified by their proper names throughout and are always labeled with a (P) or (D).

Issue: The issue is a concise question that brings out the essence of the opinion as it relates to the section of the casebook in which the case appears. Both substantive and procedural issues are included if relevant to the decision.

Palsgraf v. Long Island R.R. Co.

Injured bystander (P) v. Railroad company (D)

N.Y. Ct. App., 248 N.Y. 339, 162 N.E. 99 (1928).

NATURE OF CASE: Appeal from judgment affirming verdict for plaintiff seeking damages for personal injury.

FACT SUMMARY: Helen Palsgraf (P) was injured on R.R.'s (D) train platform when R.R.'s (D) guard helped a passenger aboard a moving train, causing his package to fall on the tracks. The package contained fireworks which exploded, creating a shock that tipped a scale onto Palsgraf (P).

RULE OF LAW

The risk reasonably to be perceived defines the duty to be obeyed.

FACTS: Helen Palsgraf (P) purchased a ticket to Rockaway Beach from R.R. (D) and was waiting on the train platform. As she waited, two men ran to catch a train that was pulling out from the platform. The first man jumped aboard, but the second man, who appeared as if he might fall, was helped aboard by the guard on the train who had kept the door open so they could jump aboard. A guard on the platform also helped by pushing him onto the train. The man was carrying a package wrapped in newspaper. In the process, the man dropped his package, which fell on the tracks. The package contained fireworks and exploded. The shock of the explosion was apparently of great enough strength to tip over some scales at the other end of the platform, which fell on Palsgraf (P) and injured her. A jury awarded her damages, and R.R. (D) appealed.

ISSUE: Does the risk reasonably to be perceived define the duty to be obeyed?

HOLDING AND DECISION: (Cardozo, C.J.) Yes. The risk reasonably to be perceived defines the duty to be obeyed. If there is no foreseeable hazard to the injured party as the result of a seemingly innocent act, the act does not become a tort because it happened to be a wrong as to another. If the wrong was not willful, the plaintiff must show that the act as to her had such great and apparent possibilities of danger as to entitle her to protection. Negligence in the abstract is not enough upon which to base liability. Negligence is a relative concept, evolving out of the common law doctrine of trespass on the case. To establish liability, the defendant must owe a legal duty of reasonable care to the injured party. A cause of action in tort will lie where harm, though unintended, could have been averted or avoided by observance of such a duty. The scope of the duty is limited by the range of danger that a reasonable person could foresee. In this case, there was nothing to suggest from the appearance of the parcel or otherwise that the parcel contained fireworks. The guard could not reasonably have had any warning of a threat to Palsgraf (P), and R.R. (D) therefore cannot be held liable. Judgment is reversed in favor of R.R. (D).

DISSENT: (Andrews, J.) The concept that there is no negligence unless R.R. (D) owes a legal duty to take care as to Palsgraf (P) herself is too narrow. Everyone owes to the world at large the duty of refraining from those acts that may unreasonably threaten the safety of others. If the guard's action was negligent as to those nearby, it was also negligent as to those outside what might be termed the "danger zone." For Palsgraf (P) to recover, R.R.'s (D) negligence must have been the proximate cause of her injury, a question of fact for the jury.

ANALYSIS

The majority defined the limit of the defendant's liability in terms of the danger that a reasonable person in defendant's situation would have perceived. The dissent argued that the limitation should not be placed on liability, but rather on damages. Judge Andrews suggested that only injuries that would not have happened but for R.R.'s (D) negligence should be compensable. Both the majority and dissent recognized the policy-driven need to limit liability for negligent acts, seeking, in the words of Judge Andrews, to define a framework "that will be practical and in keeping with the general understanding of mankind." The Restatement (Second) of Torts has accepted Judge Cardozo's view.

Quicknotes

FORESEEABILITY A reasonable expectation that change is the probable result of certain acts or omissions.

NEGLIGENCE Conduct falling below the standard of care that a reasonable person would demonstrate under similar conditions.

PROXIMATE CAUSE The natural sequence of events without which an injury would not have been sustained.

Concurrence/Dissent: All concurrences and dissents are briefed whenever they are included by the casebook author.

Analysis: This last paragraph gives you a broad understanding of where the case "fits in" with other cases in the section of the book and with the entire course. It is a hornbook-style discussion indicating whether the case is a majority or minority opinion and comparing the principal case with other cases in the casebook. It may also provide analysis from restatements, uniform codes, and law review articles.

Holding and Decision: This section offers a clear and in-depth discussion of the rule of the case and the court's rationale. It is written in easy-to-understand language and answers the issue presented by applying the law to the facts of the case. When relevant, it includes a thorough discussion of the exceptions to the case as listed by the court, any major cites to the other cases on point, and the names of the judges who wrote the decisions.

Quicknotes: Conveniently defines legal terms found in the case.

Note to Students

Aspen Publishing is proud to offer *Casenote® Legal Briefs*—continuing thirty years of publishing America's best-selling legal briefs.

Casenote® Legal Briefs are designed to help you save time when briefing assigned cases. Organized under convenient headings, they show you how to abstract the basic facts and holdings from the text of the actual opinions handed down by the courts. Used as part of a rigorous study regimen, they can help you spend more time analyzing and critiquing points of law than on copying bits and pieces of judicial opinions into your notebook or outline.

Casenote® Legal Briefs should never be used as a substitute for assigned casebook readings. They work best when read as a follow-up to reviewing the underlying opinions themselves. Students who try to avoid reading and digesting the judicial opinions in their casebooks or online sources will end up shortchanging themselves in the long run. The ability to absorb, critique, and restate the dynamic and complex elements of case law decisions is crucial to your success in law school and beyond. It cannot be developed vicariously.

In addition to *Casenote® Legal Briefs*, Aspen Publishing offers the following study aids:

- *Casenote® Legal Briefs*
- *Emanuel® Law Outlines*
- Emanuel® *Law in a Flash Flash Cards*
- Emanuel® *CrunchTime® Series*

Each of these series is designed to provide you with easy-to-understand explanations of complex points of law. Each volume offers guidance on the principles of legal analysis and, consulted regularly, will hone your ability to spot relevant issues. We have titles that will help you prepare for class, prepare for your exams, and enhance your general comprehension of the law along the way.

To find out more about our law school tools for success, visit us at *www.AspenPublishing.com* or e-mail us at *customer.service@aspenpublishing.com*. We'll be happy to assist you.

How to Brief a Case

A. Decide on a Format and Stick to It

Structure is essential to a good brief. It enables you to arrange systematically the related parts that are scattered throughout most cases, thus making manageable and understandable what might otherwise seem to be an endless and unfathomable sea of information. There are, of course, an unlimited number of formats that can be utilized. However, it is best to find one that suits your needs and stick to it. Consistency breeds both efficiency and the security that when called upon you will know where to look in your brief for the information you are asked to give.

Any format, as long as it presents the essential elements of a case in an organized fashion, can be used. Experience, however, has led *Casenote® Legal Briefs* to develop and utilize the following format because of its logical flow and universal applicability.

NATURE OF CASE: This is a brief statement of the legal character and procedural status of the case (e.g., "Appeal of a burglary conviction").

There are many different alternatives open to a litigant dissatisfied with a court ruling. The key to determining which one has been used is to discover *who is asking this court for what.*

This first entry in the brief should be kept as *short as possible.* Use the court's terminology if you understand it. But since jurisdictions vary as to the titles of pleadings, the best entry is the one that addresses who wants what in this proceeding, not the one that sounds most like the court's language.

RULE OF LAW: A statement of the general principle of law that the case illustrates (e.g., "An acceptance that varies any term of the offer is considered a rejection and counteroffer").

Determining the rule of law of a case is a procedure similar to determining the issue of the case. Avoid being fooled by red herrings; there may be a few rules of law mentioned in the case excerpt, but usually only one is *the* rule with which the casebook editor is concerned. The techniques used to locate the issue, described below, may also be utilized to find the rule of law. Generally, your best guide is simply the chapter heading. It is a clue to the point the casebook editor seeks to make and should be kept in mind when reading every case in the respective section.

FACTS: A synopsis of only the essential facts of the case, i.e., those bearing upon or leading up to the issue.

The facts entry should be a short statement of the events and transactions that led one party to initiate legal proceedings against another in the first place. While some cases conveniently state the salient facts at the beginning of the decision, in other instances they will have to be culled from hiding places throughout the text, even from concurring and dissenting opinions. Some of the "facts" will often be in dispute and should be so noted. Conflicting evidence may be briefly pointed up. "Hard" facts must be included. Both must be *relevant* in order to be listed in the facts entry. It is impossible to tell what is relevant until the entire case is read, as the ultimate determination of the rights and liabilities of the parties may turn on something buried deep in the opinion.

Generally, the facts entry should not be longer than three to five *short* sentences.

It is often helpful to identify the role played by a party in a given context. For example, in a construction contract case the identification of a party as the "contractor" or "builder" alleviates the need to tell that that party was the one who was supposed to have built the house.

It is always helpful, and a good general practice, to identify the "plaintiff" and the "defendant." This may seem elementary and uncomplicated, but, especially in view of the creative editing practiced by some casebook editors, it is sometimes a difficult or even impossible task. Bear in mind that the *party presently* seeking something from this court may not be the plaintiff, and that sometimes only the cross-claim of a defendant is treated in the excerpt. Confusing or misaligning the parties can ruin your analysis and understanding of the case.

ISSUE: A statement of the general legal question answered by or illustrated in the case. For clarity, the issue is best put in the form of a question capable of a "yes" or "no" answer. In reality, the issue is simply the Rule of Law put in the form of a question (e.g., "May an offer be accepted by performance?").

The major problem presented in discerning what is *the* issue in the case is that an opinion usually purports to raise and answer several questions. However, except for rare cases, only one such question is really the issue in the case. Collateral issues not necessary to the resolution of the matter in controversy are handled by the court by language known as *"obiter dictum"* or merely *"dictum."* While dicta may be included later in the brief, they have no place under the issue heading.

To find the issue, ask *who wants what* and then go on to ask *why did that party succeed or fail in getting it.* Once this is determined, the "why" should be turned into a question.

The complexity of the issues in the cases will vary, but in all cases a single-sentence question should sum up the issue. *In a few cases,* there will be two, or even more rarely, three issues of equal importance to the resolution of the case. Each should be expressed in a single-sentence question.

Since many issues are resolved by a court in coming to a final disposition of a case, the casebook editor will reproduce the portion of the opinion containing the issue or issues most relevant to the area of law under scrutiny. A noted law professor gave this advice: "Close the book; look at the title on the cover." Chances are, if it is Property, you need not concern yourself with whether, for example, the federal government's treatment of the plaintiff's land really raises a federal question sufficient to support jurisdiction on this ground in federal court.

The same rule applies to chapter headings designating sub-areas within the subjects. They tip you off as to what the text is designed to teach. The cases are arranged in a casebook to show a progression or development of the law, so that the preceding cases may also help.

It is also most important to remember to *read the notes and questions* at the end of a case to determine what the editors wanted you to have gleaned from it.

HOLDING AND DECISION: This section should succinctly explain the rationale of the court in arriving at its decision. In capsulizing the "reasoning" of the court, it should always include an application of the general rule or rules of law to the specific facts of the case. Hidden justifications come to light in this entry: the reasons for the state of the law, the public policies, the biases and prejudices, those considerations that influence the justices' thinking and, ultimately, the outcome of the case. At the end, there should be a short indication of thedisposition or procedural resolution of the case (e.g., "Decision of the trial court for Mr. Smith (P) reversed").

The foregoing format is designed to help you "digest" the reams of case material with which you will be faced in your law school career. Once mastered by practice, it will place at your fingertips the information the authors of your casebooks have sought to impart to you in case-by-case illustration and analysis.

B. Be as Economical as Possible in Briefing Cases

Once armed with a format that encourages succinctness, it is as important to be economical with regard to the time spent on the actual reading of the case as it is to be economical in the writing of the brief itself. This does not mean "skimming" a case. Rather, it means reading the case with an "eye" trained to recognize into which "section" of your brief a particular passage or line fits and having a system for quickly and precisely marking the case so that the passages fitting any one particular part of the brief can be easily identified and brought together in a concise and accurate manner when the brief is actually written.

It is of no use to simply repeat everything in the opinion of the court; record only enough information to trigger your recollection of what the court said. Nevertheless, an accurate statement of the "law of the case," i.e., the legal principle applied to the facts, is absolutely essential to class preparation and to learning the law under the case method.

To that end, it is important to develop a "shorthand" that you can use to make marginal notations. These notations will tell you at a glance in which section of the brief you will be placing that particular passage or portion of the opinion.

Some students prefer to underline all the salient portions of the opinion (with a pencil or colored underliner marker), making marginal notations as they go along. Others prefer the color-coded method of underlining, utilizing different colors of markers to underline the salient portions of the case, each separate color being used to represent a different section of the brief. For example, blue underlining could be used for passages relating to the rule of law, yellow for those relating to the issue, and green for those relating to the holding and decision, etc. While it has its advocates, thecolor-coded method can be confusing and time-consuming (all that time spent on changing colored markers). Furthermore, it can interfere with the continuity and concentration many students deem essential to the reading of a case for maximum comprehension. In the end, however, it is a matter of personal preference and style. Just remember, whatever method you use, underlining must be used sparingly or its value is lost.

If you take the marginal notation route, an efficient and easy method is to go along underlining the key portions of the case and placing in the margin alongside them the following "markers" to indicate where a particular passage or line "belongs" in the brief you will write:

N	(NATURE OF CASE)
RL	(RULE OF LAW)
I	(ISSUE)
HL	(HOLDING AND DECISION, relates to the RULE OF LAW behind the decision)
HR	(HOLDING AND DECISION, gives the RATIONALE or reasoning behind the decision)
HA	(HOLDING AND DECISION, applies the general principle(s) of law to the facts of the case to arrive at the decision)

Remember that a particular passage may well contain information necessary to more than one part of your brief, in which case you simply note that in the margin. If you are using the color-coded underlining method instead of marginal notation, simply make asterisks or checks in the margin next to the passage in question in the colors that indicate the additional sections of the brief where it might be utilized.

The economy of utilizing "shorthand" in marking cases for briefing can be maintained in the actual brief writing process itself by utilizing "law student shorthand" within the brief. There are many commonly used words and phrases for which abbreviations can be substituted in your briefs (and in your class notes also). You can develop abbreviations that are personal to you and which will save you a lot of time. A reference list of briefing abbreviations can be found on page x of this book.

C. Use Both the Briefing Process and the Brief as a Learning Tool

Now that you have a format and the tools for briefing cases efficiently, the most important thing is to make the time spent in briefing profitable to you and to make the most advantageous use of the briefs you create. Of course, the briefs are invaluable for classroom reference when you are called upon to explain or analyze a particular case. However, they are also useful in reviewing for exams. A quick glance at the fact summary should bring the case to mind, and a rereading of the rule of law should enable you to go over the underlying legal concept in your mind, how it was applied in that particular case, and how it might apply in other factual settings.

As to the value to be derived from engaging in the briefing process itself, there is an immediate benefit that arises from being forced to sift through the essential facts and reasoning from the court's opinion and to succinctly express them in your own words in your brief. The process ensures that you understand the case and the point that it illustrates, and that means you will be ready to absorb further analysis and information brought forth in class. It also ensures you will have something to say when called upon in class. The briefing process helps develop a mental agility for getting to the *gist* of a case and for identifying, expounding on, and applying the legal concepts and issues found there. The briefing process is the mental process on which you must rely in taking law school examinations; it is also the mental process upon which lawyers rely in serving their clients and in making a living.

Abbreviations for Briefs

acceptance	acp
affirmed	aff
answer	ans
assumption of risk	a/r
attorney	atty
beyond a reasonable doubt	b/r/d
bona fide purchaser	BFP
breach of contract	br/k
cause of action	c/a
common law	c/l
Constitution	Con
constitutional	con
contract	K
contributory negligence	c/n
cross	x
cross-complaint	x/c
cross-examination	x/ex
cruel and unusual punishment	c/u/p
defendant	D
dismissed	dis
double jeopardy	d/j
due process	d/p
equal protection	e/p
equity	eq
evidence	ev
exclude	exc
exclusionary rule	exc/r
felony	f/n
freedom of speech	f/s
good faith	g/f
habeas corpus	h/c
hearsay	hr
husband	H
injunction	inj
in loco parentis	ILP
inter vivos	I/v
joint tenancy	j/t
judgment	judgt
jurisdiction	jur
last clear chance	LCC
long-arm statute	LAS
majority view	maj
meeting of minds	MOM
minority view	min
Miranda rule	Mir/r
Miranda warnings	Mir/w
negligence	neg
notice	ntc
nuisance	nus
obligation	ob
obscene	obs
offer	O
offeree	OE
offeror	OR
ordinance	ord
pain and suffering	p/s
parol evidence	p/e
plaintiff	P
prima facie	p/f
probable cause	p/c
proximate cause	px/c
real property	r/p
reasonable doubt	r/d
reasonable man	r/m
rebuttable presumption	rb/p
remanded	rem
res ipsa loquitur	RIL
respondeat superior	r/s
Restatement	RS
reversed	rev
Rule Against Perpetuities	RAP
search and seizure	s/s
search warrant	s/w
self-defense	s/d
specific performance	s/p
statute	S
statute of frauds	S/F
statute of limitations	S/L
summary judgment	s/j
tenancy at will	t/w
tenancy in common	t/c
tenant	t
third party	TP
third party beneficiary	TPB
transferred intent	TI
unconscionable	uncon
unconstitutional	unconst
undue influence	u/e
Uniform Commercial Code	UCC
unilateral	uni
vendee	VE
vendor	VR
versus	v
void for vagueness	VFV
weight of authority	w/a
weight of the evidence	w/e
wife	W
with	w/
within	w/i
without	w/o
without prejudice	w/o/p
wrongful death	wr/d

Table of Cases

Note: There are no principal cases in Chapter 1 of the casebook.

CHAPTER 2

Relevance

Quick Reference Rules of Law

	PAGE
1. *Old Chief v. United States (I).* Relevant evidence may be excluded when its risk of unfair prejudice substantially outweighs its probative value judged in the context of the availability of alternative evidence on the same point.	2
2. *State v. Chapple.* Inflammatory evidence should not be admitted if not probative of any contested issue in the case.	3
3. *Old Chief v. United States (II).* In determining whether to admit evidence under the balancing test of Fed. R. Evid. 403, the court must weigh the probative value of the evidence sought to be admitted against the risk of unfair prejudice in light of the entire evidentiary record.	4
4. *People v. Collins.* Applications of mathematical techniques in the proof of facts in a criminal case must be critically examined in view of the substantial unfairness to the defendant that may result.	5

Old Chief v. United States (I)

Convicted felon (D) v. Federal government (P)

519 U.S. 172 (1997)

NATURE OF CASE: Appeal from conviction for possession of firearm.

FACT SUMMARY: Old Chief (D) offered to stipulate to a prior felony conviction to avoid admitting the full record of his prior offense when he was charged with violation of a statute prohibiting the possession of firearms.

RULE OF LAW

Relevant evidence may be excluded when its risk of unfair prejudice substantially outweighs its probative value judged in the context of the availability of alternative evidence on the same point.

FACTS: Old Chief (D) was charged with violation of a statute that prohibited the possession of a firearm by anyone convicted of a crime punishable by imprisonment exceeding one year. Old Chief (D) had a previous felony conviction for assault that fell within the purview of the statute. At trial, Old Chief (D) moved to exclude the name and nature of his prior conviction in exchange for a stipulation that he had been convicted of a crime punishable by imprisonment exceeding one year. The trial judge refused Old Chief's (D) stipulation, and the jury convicted him on all counts. Old Chief (D) appealed.

ISSUE: May relevant evidence be excluded when its risk of unfair prejudice substantially outweighs its probative value judged in the context of the availability of alternative evidence on the same point?

HOLDING AND DECISION: (Souter, J.) Yes. Relevant evidence may be excluded when its risk of unfair prejudice substantially outweighs its probative value judged in the context of the availability of alternative evidence on the same point. Although the prosecution is entitled to prove its case by the evidence of its own choice, this rule has no application where the evidence is not essential in providing a continuous story of its case against the defendant. The proper test is to balance the degrees of probative value and unfair prejudice for the evidence in question and for alternative, relevant evidence. The alternative evidence may be admitted if it carries the same or greater probative value, but a lower risk of unfair prejudice than the evidence in question. Reversed.

ANALYSIS

The term "unfair prejudice" speaks to the capacity of some concededly relevant evidence to lure the fact finder into declaring guilt on a ground different from proof specific to the offense charged. In other words, a defendant's earlier bad act may be generalized into bad character, thereby raising the odds that the defendant did the act the defendant is charged with. Even worse, some juries might feel justified in practicing "preventive conviction," even if they believe the defendant is momentarily innocent.

Quicknotes

PROBATIVE Tending to establish proof.

RELEVANCE The admissibility of evidence based on whether it has any tendency to prove or disprove a matter at issue to the case.

UNFAIR PREJUDICE Risk that a defendant will be convicted based on an improper reason.

State v. Chapple

Government (P) v. Convicted murderer (D)

Ariz. Sup. Ct., 660 P.2d 1208 (1983)

NATURE OF CASE: Appeal of conviction for first-degree murder.

FACT SUMMARY: A trial court admitted inflammatory evidence that was not probative of any contested issue in the case.

RULE OF LAW

Inflammatory evidence should not be admitted if not probative of any contested issue in the case.

FACTS: Chapple (D) was charged with first-degree murder in the shooting death of Varnes. Chapple (D) did not contest the identity of the victim or the cause of death. The only matter Chapple (D) contested was his identification by two eyewitnesses. At trial, the State (P) offered various color photographs of the victim's body. The photos were of a gruesome nature. The photos were not probative as to the eyewitness identification issue. The photos were admitted, and Chapple (D) was convicted. He appealed.

ISSUE: Should inflammatory evidence be admitted if not probative of any contested issue in the case?

HOLDING AND DECISION: (Feldman, J.) No. Inflammatory evidence should not be admitted if not probative of any contested issue in the case. When proffered evidence is of an inflammatory nature, the usual rule that all evidence is admissible if relevant is not necessarily followed. Even if a court determines that the evidence is relevant, it must weigh the probative value of the evidence against its prejudicial effect. When the evidence is not probative of any contested issue, its probative value is minimal, and it should be excluded. Here, the only issue was identification of the perpetrator, and the photographs were not probative of this issue. They should have been excluded. Reversed.

ANALYSIS

This rule is fairly consistent throughout the various jurisdictions. It is codified in Fed. R. Evid. 403. Although the trial court in this case was reversed, much discretion is usually left to the court.

Quicknotes

PROBATIVE Tending to establish proof.

RELEVANCE The admissibility of evidence based on whether it has any tendency to prove or disprove a matter at issue to the case.

Old Chief v. United States (II)

Convicted felon (D) v. Federal government (P)

519 U.S. 172 (1997)

NATURE OF CASE: Appeal from charge of being a felon in possession of a firearm and assault with a dangerous weapon.

FACT SUMMARY: Old Chief (D) offered to stipulate to a prior felony conviction to avoid admitting the full record of his prior offense when he was charged with violation of a statute prohibiting the possession of firearms.

RULE OF LAW

In determining whether to admit evidence under the balancing test of Fed. R. Evid. 403, the court must weigh the probative value of the evidence sought to be admitted against the risk of unfair prejudice in light of the entire evidentiary record.

FACTS: Old Chief (D) was charged with violation of a statute that prohibited the possession of a firearm by anyone convicted of a crime punishable by imprisonment exceeding one year. Old Chief (D) had a previous felony conviction of assault that fell within the purview of the statute. At trial, Old Chief (D) moved to exclude the name and nature of his prior conviction in exchange for a stipulation that he had been convicted of a crime punishable by imprisonment exceeding one year. The trial judge refused Old Chief's (D) stipulation, and the jury convicted him on all counts. Old Chief (D) appealed.

ISSUE: In determining whether to admit evidence under the balancing test of Fed. R. Evid. 403, must the court weigh any probative value the evidence sought to be admitted might have against the risk of unfair prejudice in light of the entire evidentiary record?

HOLDING AND DECISION: (Souter, J.) Yes. In determining whether to admit evidence under the balancing test of Fed. R. Evid. 403, the court must weigh the probative value of the evidence sought to be admitted against the risk of unfair prejudice in light of the entire evidentiary record. In balancing the probative value of the evidence against the risk of unfair prejudice under Fed. R. Evid. 403, there are two possibilities. Either the item of evidence may be considered alone, or it may be considered in context of the totality of the evidentiary record. If an objection is raised, then the court must decide whether the particular item presents a danger of unfair prejudice. If so, the judge must evaluate the degrees of probative value and unfair prejudice for the item or any available substitutes. Where its probative value is substantially outweighed by unfair prejudicial risk, then the item will be disclosed. Under this approach a defendant's Fed. R. Evid. 403 objection offering to concede a point would not prevail over the prosecution's decision to offer evidence of guilt and all the circumstances surrounding the offense. The commentary to Fed. R. Evid. 403 makes it clear that the term "probative value" refers to the consideration of one item of evidence while the term "relevance" involves the comparison of evidentiary alternatives. The comments also state that a party's concession is relevant to the court's discretion to exclude evidence relating to the point conceded. Such decisions are to be made on the bases of expedience and undue prejudice, not relevance. Moreover, the comments state that in making such a ruling the court may consider the availability of alternative means of proof. Evidence of the name or nature of a prior offense normally risks unfair prejudice to the defendant. Here, as in any other case in which a prior conviction is likely to support a conviction on an improper ground, the risk of unfair prejudice outweighed the probative value of the conviction record. The court abused its discretion in admitting the record when an admission was available. Reversed and remanded.

DISSENT: (O'Connor, J.) Here, one is not found guilty of a crime or felony but of "a specified offense." Troubling is the majority's argument that the general principle favoring evidentiary depth has "virtually no application" in this case since a jury is "as likely to be puzzled" by a "missing chapter" relating to a prior felony conviction as it would be by a concession of any other element in the crime.

ANALYSIS

Note that the Court limited its holding to actions that involve proof that the defendant is a felon. Generally, appellate review of a decision under Fed. R. Evid. 403 requires the defendant to demonstrate the lower court abused its discretion in admitting or not admitting the evidence. This requires a greater showing than mere proof of alternative evidence.

Quicknotes

PROBATIVE Tending to establish proof.

RELEVANCE The admissibility of evidence based on whether it has any tendency to prove or disprove a matter at issue to the case.

People v. Collins

Government (P) v. Convicted robber (D)

Cal. Sup. Ct., 438 P.2d 33 (1968)

NATURE OF CASE: Appeal from conviction of second-degree robbery.

FACT SUMMARY: In the People's (P) suit against Collins (D) for second-degree armed robbery, Collins (D) contended that testimony admitted into evidence at trial as to the mathematical probability that Collins (D) committed the crime unduly influenced the jury and infected the case with fatal error.

RULE OF LAW

Applications of mathematical techniques in the proof of facts in a criminal case must be critically examined in view of the substantial unfairness to the defendant that may result.

FACTS: In the People's (P) suit against Collins (D) for second-degree robbery, the prosecution experienced some difficulty in establishing the perpetrators of the robbery. In order to bolster the identification of Collins (D) as the perpetrator, the prosecutor called a mathematics instructor from a state college who testified about the mathematical probability that persons who possessed the various characteristics possessed by Collins (D) and his wife, a co-defendant, existed. The witness inferred that there could be but one chance in twelve million that Collins (D) and his wife (D) were innocent and that another equally distinctive couple actually committed the robbery. Collins (D) objected to the witness's testimony on the grounds that it was based on unfounded assumptions. Collins (D) was convicted and appealed on the grounds the mathematician's testimony infected the case with fatal error.

ISSUE: Must applications of mathematical techniques in the proof of facts in a criminal case be critically examined in view of the substantial unfairness to the defendant that may result?

HOLDING AND DECISION: (Sullivan, J.) Yes. Application of mathematical techniques in the proof of facts in a criminal case must be critically examined in view of the substantial unfairness to the defendant that may result. Here, the prosecution's theory of probability rested on the assumption that the witness called by the People (P) had conclusively established that the guilty couple possessed the precise characteristics relied upon by the prosecution. But no mathematical formula could ever establish beyond a reasonable doubt that the prosecution's witness correctly observed and accurately described the distinctive features that were employed to link the Collinses (D) to the crime. The most a mathematical computation could ever yield would be a measure of the probability that a random couple would possess the distinctive features in question. Reversed.

ANALYSIS

It appears that the explicit use of theories of probability and statistical inference remains controversial. This is true whether the theories serve either as a basis for the opinions of the experts themselves or as a course of education for jurors in how to think about scientific identification evidence. However, so as long as counsel and the experts do not try to place a scientific seal of approval on results not shown to be grounded in science, there is probably room for judicious use of these theories to put identification evidence in perspective.

CHAPTER 3

Hearsay

Quick Reference Rules of Law

Wright v. Doe d. Tatham

Steward (D) v. Cousin of deceased (P)

Ex., 7 Ad. & E. 313, 112 Eng. Rep. 488 (1837)

NATURE OF CASE: Appeal from order validating a will.

FACT SUMMARY: Tatham (P) contended letters written to the testator Marsden were admissible to prove the mental capacity of Marsden at the time the will was made.

RULE OF LAW

Hearsay statements offered to establish a fact based upon the opinion of the declarant are inadmissible.

FACTS: Marsden died testate leaving valuable property to his steward, Wright (D). Tatham (P), Marsden's cousin, sued to invalidate the will, contending Marsden lacked mental capacity to affect a valid will. Wright (D) introduced two letters written by different individuals to Marsden relating to various legal matters. The purpose of these letters was to establish that the writers of the letters considered Marsden legally competent to attend to his own affairs. Based in part upon these letters, which were entered into evidence, the will was upheld. Tatham (P) appealed, contending the content of the letters, offered to prove the mental capacity of the person to whom they were written, was inadmissible hearsay.

ISSUE: Are hearsay statements offered to establish a fact based upon the opinion of the declarant admissible?

HOLDING AND DECISION: (Baron Parke, J.) No. Hearsay statements offered to establish a fact based upon the opinion of the declarant are inadmissible. The statements contained in the letters were made outside of court and were offered to prove the truth of the statements. The purpose behind the introduction of the statements into evidence was to show the declarant felt that the person to whom the letters were written, Marsden, had the legal capacity to understand and carry on his own affairs. These facts were relevant only as implying a statement or opinion of a third person on a matter in issue and are thus inadmissible where such statement or opinion would of itself be inadmissible. The declarants or writers of the letters could not have come into court to testify that they made the statements previously, due to the hearsay rule. As a result, the letters were inadmissible.

ANALYSIS

This case represents an excellent example of nonassertive conduct as hearsay. The statements in the letters themselves were not necessarily offered on face value to prove their truth. It was what was to be implied from the statements that did not offer the requisite level of reliability to allow them to overcome the hearsay prohibition. The court likened the written statements to spoken words that if offered for their truth would likewise be inadmissible hearsay.

Quicknotes

HEARSAY An out-of-court statement made by a person other than the witness testifying at trial that is offered in order to prove the truth of the matter asserted.

Cain v. George

Parents of deceased child (P) v. Hotel owner (D)

411 F.2d 572 (5th Cir. 1969)

NATURE OF CASE: Appeal of denial of damages for wrongful death.

FACT SUMMARY: A trial court admitted evidence of a lack of prior complaints about an allegedly defective heater.

RULE OF LAW

Evidence regarding complaints is not hearsay.

FACTS: The Cains' (P) child was found dead in a hotel room. He was lying near a smoldering chair that was adjacent to a heater. The cause of death was carbon monoxide poisoning. The Cains (P) sued, contending that the source of the gas was the heater. George (D), the hotel owner, contended this was not so. The trial court permitted George (D) to testify, over the Cains' (P) hearsay objection, that there had been no prior complaints regarding the heater. The jury rendered a defense verdict, and the Cains (P) appealed.

ISSUE: Is evidence regarding complaints hearsay?

HOLDING AND DECISION: (Per curiam) No. Evidence regarding complaints is not hearsay. Such evidence is not dependent on the veracity and credibility of the would-be declarants, but rather on that of the testifying witness. This being so, the policy implications of hearsay do not arise and excluding such evidence is not proper. Affirmed.

ANALYSIS

The rule might be different if evidence regarding complaints, as opposed to a lack of complaints, was at issue. In that case, out-of-court statements would be sought as an admission. Whether such statements would be classified hearsay is debatable; also, there is a good chance an exception, such as for business records, could be found.

Quicknotes

HEARSAY An out-of-court statement made by a person other than the witness testifying at trial that is offered in order to prove the truth of the matter asserted.

United States v. Check

Federal government (P) v. Convicted drug-dealing police officer (D)

582 F.2d 668 (2d Cir. 1978)

NATURE OF CASE: Appeal from conviction of possession of cocaine with intent to distribute.

FACT SUMMARY: In a prosecution based on possession of cocaine, the State (P) attempted to circumvent the hearsay rule by suggesting what an unavailable declarant said.

RULE OF LAW

The hearsay rule cannot be circumvented by framing testimony so as to suggest what an unavailable declarant said.

FACTS: As part of an internal investigation of police officer Check (D), undercover officer Spinelli had dealings with one Cali, who made statements tending to incriminate Check (D). Check (D) was charged with possession of cocaine with intent to distribute. Cali was unavailable to testify. The Government (P) elicited testimony from Spinelli, on direct, as to his conversations with Cali. While Spinelli did not quote Cali, he quoted his responses to Cali, responses that suggested what Cali had said. Check (D) was convicted, and he appealed.

ISSUE: Can the hearsay rule be circumvented by framing testimony so as to suggest what an unavailable declarant said?

HOLDING AND DECISION: (Waterman, J.) No. The hearsay rule cannot be circumvented by framing testimony so to suggest what an unavailable declarant said. When testimony is framed so as to lead to out-of-court statements being introduced to prove their own truth, the hearsay rule is invoked, even if the statements are not directly quoted. This was the case here. In substance, Cali's statements were introduced although they were not introduced verbatim. Reversed and remanded.

ANALYSIS

The case stands for the proposition that hearsay can be a subtle thing. Often, words or acts will suggest something that is itself hearsay. Unless a reason to introduce the words or acts for something other than the hearsay purpose can be found, exclusion is proper.

Quicknotes

HEARSAY An out-of-court statement made by a person other than the witness testifying at trial that is offered in order to prove the truth of the matter asserted.

United States v. Singer

Federal government (P) v. Convicted drug dealer (D)

687 F.2d 1135, modified, 710 F.2d 431 (8th Cir. 1983)

NATURE OF CASE: Appeal of conviction for drug-related offenses.

FACT SUMMARY: Sazenski (D) raised a hearsay objection to the introduction of evidence of conduct not intended as an assertion.

RULE OF LAW

Evidence of conduct not intended as an assertion of fact is not made inadmissible by the hearsay rule.

FACTS: Sazenski (D) and Izquierdo (D) roomed together. Izquierdo (D) used the alias "Carlos Almaden." They were prosecuted for various drug-related offenses. At one point, the Government (P) introduced a letter addressed to Sazenski (D) and "Carlos Almaden" to prove they shared a residence. Sazenski's (D) hearsay objection was overruled. Sazenski (D) was convicted, and he appealed.

ISSUE: Is evidence of conduct not intended as an assertion of fact made inadmissible by the hearsay rule?

HOLDING AND DECISION: (Henley, J.) No. Evidence of conduct not intended as an assertion of fact is not made inadmissible by the hearsay rule. When evidence of conduct tends to demonstrate behavior based on a belief, the untrustworthiness implications of the hearsay rule are not brought into play. People tend to conform their behavior to their beliefs. Here, the writer of the letter addressed it as he did because of a belief that Sazenski (D) and "Carlos Almaden" lived at that address together. Evidence of this was not hearsay. Affirmed.

ANALYSIS

"Hearsay" is defined only to include "statements." Technically, behavior is not a statement. However, it has been established for a long time that conduct can be, if conditions are met, tantamount to verbal assertions for purposes of the hearsay.

Quicknotes

HEARSAY An out-of-court statement made by a person other than the witness testifying at trial that is offered in order to prove the truth of the matter asserted.

United States v. Pacelli

Federal government (P) v. Convicted murderer (D)

491 F.2d 1108 (2d Cir.), *cert. denied*, 419 U.S. 826 (1974)

NATURE OF CASE: Appeal of a conviction for civil rights violation.

FACT SUMMARY: Pacelli (D) raised a hearsay objection to the introduction of statements implying facts asserted to prove their own truth.

RULE OF LAW

Testimony regarding statements that imply facts presented to prove their own truth is hearsay.

FACTS: Pacelli (D) was charged with violating the civil rights of Parks, whom he allegedly murdered. At trial, the Government (P) introduced certain statements of associates of Pacelli (D) that, although not directly saying that Pacelli (D) committed the murder, clearly implied this belief. Pacelli's (D) hearsay objection was overruled. He was convicted, and he appealed.

ISSUE: Is testimony regarding statements that imply facts presented to prove their own truth hearsay?

HOLDING AND DECISION: (Mansfield, J.) Yes. Testimony regarding statements that imply facts presented to prove their own truth is hearsay. When extra-judicial statements imply knowledge and belief on the part of nontestifying declarants as to material facts and are introduced to prove their own truth, the hearsay rule is directly implicated. Here, the statements made by the nontestifying declarants implied belief that Pacelli (D) committed the murder, and no purpose other than establishing this fact was served by the statements' introduction. This was clearly a hearsay violation. Reversed and remanded.

DISSENT: (Moore, J.) As no declarant actually expressed an opinion that Pacelli (D) committed the murder, the hearsay rule was not implicated.

ANALYSIS

The opinion and dissent basically disagree as to how far the hearsay rule may go. The dissent would limit it to actual assertions. The majority was of the view that the rule could be invoked when the fact in question is merely implied.

Quicknotes

HEARSAY An out-of-court statement made by a person other than the witness testifying at trial that is offered in order to prove the truth of the matter asserted.

Betts v. Betts

Father (P) v. Mother (D)

Wash. Ct. App., 473 P.2d 403 (1970)

NATURE OF CASE: Appeal of child custody order.

FACT SUMMARY: In a custody hearing, the court admitted testimony regarding statements by the child that were relevant whether or not they were true.

RULE OF LAW
Statements that are relevant whether they are true or not do not implicate the hearsay rule.

FACTS: Rita Betts (D), after divorcing Michael Betts (P), was awarded custody of their children. Rita (D) began living with Caporale. Not long after, one of the children died from severe injuries. Caporale was tried for murder and acquitted. The other child was placed in a foster home. Michael (P) commenced a custody proceeding. At the proceeding, the foster mother testified as to the child's statements that Caporale had killed her brother and would kill her as well. Rita's (D) hearsay objection was overruled. Michael (P) was awarded custody, and Rita (D) appealed.

ISSUE: Do statements that are relevant whether they are true or not implicate the hearsay rule?

HOLDING AND DECISION: (Armstrong, C.J.) No. Statements that are relevant whether they are true or not do not implicate the hearsay rule. The rule relates to out-of-court statements that are admitted to prove their own truth. When the statements are relevant, whether or not they are true, the rule necessarily is inapplicable. Here, the testimony regarding the child's statements was relevant to the issue of how being placed in the same house as Caporale would affect her. Whether her beliefs in this regard were true would be largely irrelevant as to this issue, and therefore the statements were not hearsay. Affirmed.

ANALYSIS

Because the statements by the child were held not to be hearsay, the necessity of discussing exceptions thereto did not arise. Several exceptions probably could have been found had this been necessary. The most obvious would have been the "state-of-mind" exception. The "excited utterance" exception might also apply.

Quicknotes

EXCITED UTTERANCE An exception to the hearsay rule for statements made or caused by the happening of a startling occurrence and that are related to that occurrence.

HEARSAY An out-of-court statement made by a person other than the witness testifying at trial that is offered in order to prove the truth of the matter asserted.

STATE-OF-MIND EXCEPTION An exception to the hearsay rule for the admission of an out-of-court declaration to prove the declarant's present reason for action despite the declarant's unavailability.

CHAPTER 4

Hearsay Exceptions

Quick Reference Rules of Law

State v. Smith

State (P) v. Convicted assailant (D)

Wash. Sup. Ct., 651 P.2d 207 (1982)

NATURE OF CASE: Appeal of order granting new trial following conviction for assault.

FACT SUMMARY: A sworn statement by assault victim Conlin was admitted as an inconsistent statement after she refused, at trial, to identify Smith (D) as her attacker, as she had earlier done.

RULE OF LAW

A sworn statement inconsistent with courtroom testimony may be substantively introduced if reliable.

FACTS: Conlin was assaulted and severely battered in a motel room. Initially she identified Smith (D), with whom she lived, as the assailant. She wrote out a statement identifying him as the perpetrator, and then signed it under penalty of perjury. At trial, however, she changed her testimony and stated that another man was responsible. The trial court permitted the prosecution to introduce the statement substantively, over Smith's (D) hearsay objection. Smith (D) was convicted. The court, changing its mind regarding the admissibility of the statement, ordered a new trial. The prosecution appealed.

ISSUE: May a sworn statement inconsistent with courtroom testimony be substantively introduced if reliable?

HOLDING AND DECISION: (Dimmick, J.) Yes. A sworn statement inconsistent with courtroom testimony may be substantively introduced if reliable. Fed. R. Evid. 801(d)(1)(A), adopted in the State of Washington, permits the substantive introduction of prior inconsistent statements if given under oath at a trial, hearing, deposition, or "other proceeding." What constitutes an "other proceeding" is not defined. The usual approach, which this court adopts, is to analyze each situation on an ad hoc basis to decide on admissibility. Reliability is the key. Here, the inconsistent statement was made while the incident was fresh in Conlin's mind, before she had a chance to forget or be intimidated into changing her story. This demonstrates reliability on the part of the statement, and its admission was proper. Reversed and remanded.

ANALYSIS

The present form of Fed. R. Evid. 801(d)(1)(A) came about as a compromise. The Senate version would have permitted the substantive admission of all inconsistent statements. The House versions would have permitted only those made in grand jury proceedings.

Quicknotes

HEARSAY An out-of-court statement made by a person other than the witness testifying at trial that is offered in order to prove the truth of the matter asserted.

State v. Motta

State (P) v. Convicted robber (D)

Haw. Sup. Ct., 659 P.2d 745 (1983)

NATURE OF CASE: Appeal of conviction for robbery.

FACT SUMMARY: Motta (D) was convicted of robbery after a composite sketch was admitted into evidence.

RULE OF LAW

A composite sketch is not made inadmissible by the hearsay rule.

FACTS: Iwashita was robbed at gunpoint. Soon thereafter, based on her description of the perpetrator, a composite sketch was made by a police artist. Iwashita later picked out Motta's (D) photo from a series of mug shots. At trial, Iwashita identified Motta (D) as the assailant. The sketch was admitted as substantive evidence over Motta's (D) hearsay objection. Motta (D) was convicted, and he appealed.

ISSUE: Is a composite sketch made inadmissible by the hearsay rule?

HOLDING AND DECISION: (Lum, C.J.) No. A composite sketch is not made inadmissible by the hearsay rule. Some courts have declined to consider such evidence as hearsay. This court is not so inclined because such a sketch is properly considered the product of out-of-court statements whose only relevance is their own truth. However, Fed. R. Evid. 801(d)(1)(C), adopted in this state, permits the substantive introduction of prior identifications as a hearsay exception, as long as the identifying individual is available for cross-examination. As the sketch was a result of identification and both Iwashita and the artist were available, the requirements of the rule were met. Affirmed.

ANALYSIS

Motta (D) argued that the sketch was in essence a corroboration of Iwashita's testimony. Such evidence, argued Motta (D), should be admitted only to rebut impeaching evidence, of which none existed. The court rejected this, holding that the sketch was substantively admissible and not merely a vehicle for rehabilitation.

Quicknotes

CROSS-EXAMINATION The interrogation of a witness by an adverse party either to further inquire as to the subject matter of the direct examination or to call into question the witness's credibility.

HEARSAY RULE Rule that an out-of-court statement made by a person other than the witness testifying at trial and that is offered in order to prove the truth of the matter asserted is inadmissible.

Bruton v. United States

Convicted robber (D) v. Federal government (P)

391 U.S. 123 (1968)

NATURE OF CASE: Appeal from conviction for robbery.

FACT SUMMARY: The Government (P) contended that Bruton's (D) robbery conviction based upon the confession of a co-conspirator was valid.

RULE OF LAW

In a joint trial with two co-defendants, it is improper to admit into evidence one co-defendant's confession that implicates the second co-defendant, even if there is an instruction to the jury that it should only consider the confession as evidence against the defendant who made the statement.

FACTS: Evans was arrested and charged with armed postal robbery. In the course of his confinement, he orally confessed to the postal authorities that both he and Bruton (D) committed the robbery. A joint trial was held wherein Evans's confession was admitted into evidence. The court instructed the jury that while the confession was substantive evidence against Evans, it could not be used to determine the guilt of Bruton (D). Both individuals were convicted, and Evans's conviction was overturned when it was determined that his confession should not be used against him. However, Bruton's (D) conviction was affirmed based upon the trial judge's limiting instruction. Bruton (D) appealed, contending the use of the confession in a joint trial constituted reversible error as to his conviction.

ISSUE: In a joint trial with two co-defendants, is it proper to admit into evidence one co-defendant's confession that implicates the second co-defendant, even if there is an instruction to the jury that it should only consider the confession as evidence against the defendant who made the statement?

HOLDING AND DECISION: (Brennan, J.) No. In a joint trial with two co-defendants, it is improper to admit into evidence one co-defendant's confession that implicates the second co-defendant, even if there is an instruction to the jury that it should only consider the confession as evidence against the defendant who made the statement. The use of such a confession presents a substantial risk that the jury, despite the instructions to the contrary, will look to the incriminating extra-judicial statements in determining a defendant's guilt. In the case at bar, the use of the confession deprived Bruton (D) of his right of cross-examination under the Confrontation Clause of the Sixth Amendment. Although there are many circumstances in which the reliance upon the jury's following the court's order to disregard certain pieces of evidence and to use it only for particular purposes will be harmless, some pieces of evidence are so prejudicial as to require their exclusion. The risk of misuse is simply too high where such use potentially robs the co-defendant of his or her constitutional rights. Further, the confession of a co-defendant is so lacking in reliability with regard to the nonconfessing defendant that the hearsay rule must be strictly applied. Reversed.

DISSENT: (White, J.) The practical result of the Court's opinion in this case is to severely limit the ability of prosecutors to hold joint trials for defendants. The great value in using an uncoerced admission against one defendant when that would render the co-defendant's conviction questionable will surely dissuade prosecutors from joint trials. This will greatly increase the judicial workload and the benefits of joint trials will be lost.

ANALYSIS

There is no question that the use of a co-defendant's admission against another defendant is clearly hearsay. It is an out-of-court statement offered for its truth. It also contains several elements of unreliability including the fact that it is made under a stressful condition and usually made in an attempt to exalt the declarant at the expense of the co-defendant. As a result of this unreliability, the court is unwilling to allow it into evidence at all in a joint trial. Even though, as the dissent points out, there are great benefits to using an uncoerced confession against the declarant, many commentators have indicated that this benefit is clearly outweighed by the risk of the non-declarant defendant's loss of his constitutional rights.

Quicknotes

CROSS-EXAMINATION The interrogation of a witness by an adverse party either to further inquire as to the subject matter of the direct examination or to call into question the witness's credibility.

HEARSAY RULE Rule that an out-of-court statement made by a person other than the witness testifying at trial and that is offered in order to prove the truth of the matter asserted is inadmissible.

REVERSIBLE ERROR A substantial error that might reasonably have prejudiced the party complaining.

SIXTH AMENDMENT Provides the right to a speedy and public trial by impartial jury, the right to be informed of the accusation, the right to confront witnesses, and the right to have the assistance of counsel in all criminal prosecutions.

United States v. Hoosier

Federal government (P) v. Convicted robber (D)

542 F.2d 687 (1976)

NATURE OF CASE: Appeal from a conviction for armed robbery.

FACT SUMMARY: A witness at Hoosier's (D) trial for armed robbery was permitted to testify to certain statements Hoosier's (D) girlfriend had made in Hoosier's (D) presence and to which he had offered no denial.

RULE OF LAW

The hearsay exception for an admission by a party opponent applies when the statement offered is against a party who manifested his or her adoption of or belief in the truth of the statement.

FACTS: Hoosier (D) was convicted of armed robbery in a trial where the court allowed a witness to testify as to certain statements by Hoosier's (D) girlfriend. Hoosier (D) argued the statements constituted inadmissible hearsay. The witness testified that he saw Hoosier (D) and his girlfriend three weeks after the robbery and that Hoosier (D) had money and was wearing diamond rings. He further testified that the girlfriend had commented on Hoosier's (D) affluence, telling the witness, "That ain't nothing, you should have seen the money we had in the hotel room," thereafter speaking of "sacks of money." In the face of these statements, Hoosier (D) made no denial or other comment.

ISSUE: Does the hearsay exception for an admission by a party opponent apply when the statement offered is against a party who manifested his or her adoption of or belief in the truth of that statement?

HOLDING AND DECISION: (Per curiam) Yes. The hearsay exception for an admission by a party opponent applies when the statement offered is against a party who manifested his or her adoption of or belief in the truth of the statement. Adoption or acquiescence in the statement of another can be manifested in any appropriate manner—including failure to protest an untrue statement made in one's presence when such a protest would normally be forthcoming under the circumstances were the statement untrue. In such case, the decision calls for an evaluation in terms of probable human behavior. In this case, there is little likelihood that Hoosier's (D) silence in the face of his girlfriend's statements was due to "advice of counsel" or assertion of his Fifth Amendment right to remain silent. Under the total circumstances, probable human behavior would have been for him to deny her statements were they not true. Thus, admission of the statements was proper. Affirmed.

ANALYSIS

Use of much of this type of evidence in criminal cases has been circumscribed by the constitutional restraints of *Miranda* and its progeny. When accusations are made, a defendant's failure to respond will usually be the result of the defendant's having been informed (1) that his or her utterances might be used against him or her, and (2) that it is his or her right to remain silent. Thus, use of this type of silence to admit such accusations would be unconstitutional.

Quicknotes

FIFTH AMENDMENT Provides that no person shall be compelled to serve as a witness against him- or herself, be subject to trial for the same offense twice, or be deprived of life, liberty, or property without due process of law.

HEARSAY RULE Rule that an out-of-court statement made by a person other than the witness testifying at trial and that is offered in order to prove the truth of the matter asserted is inadmissible.

Doyle v. Ohio

Convicted drug dealer (D) v. State (P)

426 U.S. 610 (1976)

NATURE OF CASE: Review of conviction for selling narcotics.

FACT SUMMARY: The prosecution attempted to impeach drug-offense defendant Doyle's (D) exculpatory story by noting his failure to tell the same story upon arrest.

RULE OF LAW

A state may not impeach a defendant's exculpatory story by noting his or her failure to tell the same story upon arrest.

FACTS: Through the use of a "plant," police were able to observe a purported sale of marijuana by Doyle (D), who was subsequently arrested. At trial, Doyle (D) offered an exculpatory version of events. The prosecution, upon cross-examination, inquired as to why he had not told the same story upon arrest. He had been given *Miranda* warnings. Doyle (D) was convicted, and the conviction was upheld on state appeal. The United States Supreme Court granted review.

ISSUE: May a state impeach a defendant's exculpatory story by noting his or her failure to tell the same story upon arrest?

HOLDING AND DECISION: (Powell, J.) No. A state may not impeach a defendant's exculpatory story by noting his or her failure to tell the same story upon arrest. When an arrestee, after receiving the Miranda warnings, chooses to remain silent, no inference of guilt may arise from this. To hold otherwise would make these rights meaningless. While the warning contains no express assurance that silence carries no penalty, an arrestee may properly infer this. Therefore, to permit a defendant to be cross-examined regarding post-arrest silence, as Doyle (D) was here, violates due process. Reversed and remanded.

DISSENT: (Stevens, J.) Silence in matters such as this is tantamount to a prior inconsistent statement and should be admissible as impeachment.

ANALYSIS

The key to this decision was the actual informing of the suspect that he had the right to be silent. This was tantamount to a promise that silence would place no peril upon the arrestee. The Court later, in *Jenkins v. Anderson*, 447 U.S. 231 (1980), declined to extend the rule to cover prearrest silence. Prearrest matters do not implicate the *Miranda* warning.

Quicknotes

CROSS-EXAMINATION The interrogation of a witness by an adverse party either to further inquire as to the subject matter of the direct examination or to call into question the witness's credibility.

DUE PROCESS The constitutional mandate requiring the courts to protect and enforce individuals' rights and liberties consistent with prevailing principles of fairness and justice and prohibiting the federal and state governments from such activities that deprive its citizens of life, liberty, or property interest.

IMPEACHMENT The discrediting of a witness by offering evidence to show that the witness lacks credibility.

Mahlandt v. Wild Canid Survival & Research Center

Injured child (P) v. Animal center (D)

588 F.2d 626 (8th Cir. 1978)

NATURE OF CASE: Appeal from denial of damages for negligence.

FACT SUMMARY: The trial court hearing Daniel Mahlandt's (P) civil action against the Wild Canid Survival & Research Center (the Center) (D) refused to let into evidence certain conclusionary statements against interest made by an employee of the Center (D).

RULE OF LAW

Under Fed. R. Evid. 801(d)(2)(D), statements made by an agent within the scope of the agent's employment are admissible, without an implied requirement of the declarant's personal knowledge of the facts underlying his or her statement.

FACTS: No one witnessed what happened, but young Daniel Mahlandt (P), who was just under four years old at the time, wound up in the enclosure where Kenneth Poos (D), the Director of the Wild Canid Survival & Research Center (the Center) (D), kept Sophie, a wolf belonging to the Center (D). The wolf was tame enough to take to schools and institutions where Poos (D) showed films and gave programs on the nature of wolves. Sophie had been raised at the children's zoo and demonstrated a good nature and stable manner while in contact with thousands of children. Sophie apparently bit Mahlandt (P), causing him serious injuries. There was some evidence indicating that Mahlandt (P) might have received his injuries crawling under the fence. An effort to disprove this theory was made by introducing evidence that Poos (D) had left a note on the door of the Center's (D) president saying a wolf had bitten a child and that Poos (D) had made a similar statement later that day when he met the president and was asked what happened. There was also an offer to introduce minutes of a meeting of the Center's (D) board that reflected a great deal of discussion about the legal aspects of the incident of Sophie biting the child. None of this was admitted into evidence, the judge reasoning that in each case those making the statements had no personal knowledge of the facts and the statements were thus hearsay. A judgment for the Center (D) followed.

ISSUE: Under Fed. R. Evid. 801(d)(2)(D), are statements made by an agent within the scope of the agent's employment admissible, without an implied requirement of the declarant's personal knowledge of the facts underlying his or her statement?

HOLDING AND DECISION: (Van Sickle, J.) Yes. Under Fed. R. Evid. 801(d)(2)(D) statements made by an agent within the scope of the agent's employment are admissible, without an implied requirement of the declarant's personal knowledge of the facts underlying his or her statement. Rule 403 provides for the exclusion of relevant evidence if its probative value is substantially outweighed by the danger of unfair prejudice, etc. Rule 805 recites, in effect, that a statement containing hearsay within hearsay is admissible if each part of the statement falls within an exception to the hearsay rule. While each rule provided additional bases for excluding otherwise acceptable evidence, neither rule mandates the introduction into Rule 801(d)(2)(D) of an implied requirement that the declarant have personal knowledge of the facts underlying his or her statement. Thus, the two statements made by Poos (D) (one in the note he wrote and one he made verbally) were admissible against the Center (D). As to the minutes of the Center's (D) board meeting, there was no servant or agency relationship that justified admitting the evidence of these minutes as against Poos (D) (who was a nonattending, nonparticipating employee). The only remaining question is whether the trial court's rulings excluding these three items of evidence are at all justified under Rule 403. It is true that none of the statements involved were based on the personal knowledge of the declarant. However, the Advisory Committee on Proposed Rules recognized that this does not necessarily mean they must be rejected as too unreliable to be admitted into evidence. In its discussion of 801(d)(2) exceptions to the hearsay rule, the Committee said: "The freedom which admissions have enjoyed from technical demands of searching for an assurance of trustworthiness in some against-interest circumstances, and from the restrictive influences of the opinion rule and the rule requiring first-hand knowledge, when taken with the apparently prevalent satisfaction with the results, calls for generous treatment of this avenue to admissibility." 28 U.S.C.A., Volume of Federal Rules of Evidence, Rule 801, p. 527, at p. 530. So here, remembering that relevant evidence is usually prejudicial to the cause of the side against which it is presented, and that the prejudice that concerns us is unreasonable prejudice—and applying the spirit of Rule 801(d)(2)—Rule 403 does not warrant the exclusion of the evidence of Poos's (D) statements as against himself or the Center (D). But the limited admissibility of the corporate minutes, coupled with the repetitive nature of the evidence and the low probative value of the minute record, all justify supporting the judgment of the trial court, under Rule 403, not to admit them into evidence. Reversed and remanded for a new trial.

Continued on next page.

ANALYSIS

One of the questions courts have struggled with in this area is whether or not in order to qualify as an admission, the statement must have been made by the agent to an outsider (i.e., one other than the agent's principal or another agent). This often comes up when the opposing party in a suit against the principal wants to introduce into evidence a report written or given orally by an agent to the principal or another agent. Just as many courts have refused to let such evidence in as have let it in against the principal as an admission.

Quicknotes

HEARSAY RULE Rule that an out-of-court statement made by a person other than the witness testifying at trial and that is offered in order to prove the truth of the matter asserted is inadmissible.

Nuttall v. Reading Co.

Wife of deceased (P) v. Employer (D)

235 F.2d 546 (3d Cir. 1956)

NATURE OF CASE: Appeal of directed verdict dismissing action for damages under the Federal Employers' Liability Act.

FACT SUMMARY: Nuttall (P) attempted to introduce statements made by her late husband during a telephone conversation with his employer.

RULE OF LAW

In an action based on forcing an ill employee to work, testimony regarding the employee's conversations with the employer may be admissible.

FACTS: Nuttall (P), executrix of her husband's estate, filed an action under the Federal Employers' Liability Act (FELA), against her husband's former employer, Reading Co. (D). At trial, Nuttall (P) sought to introduce testimony regarding a telephone conversation her husband had had with his supervisor on a particular day, when he had tried to phone in sick. Her husband's portion of the conversation suggested that the supervisor (who was also deceased) had forced him to come to work. The court refused the testimony and delivered a directed verdict in favor of Reading (D). Nuttall (P) appealed.

ISSUE: In an action based on forcing an ill employee to work, may testimony regarding the employee's conversations with the employer be admissible?

HOLDING AND DECISION: (Goodrich, J.) Yes. In an action based on forcing an ill employee to work, testimony regarding the employee's conversations with the employer may be admissible. An employer covered by the Federal Employers' Liability Act may be liable for forcing an ill employee to work. Liability requires proof that the employee was coerced. Testimony regarding a conversation between the employee and the employer is probative on this issue and should be admitted. Reversed and remanded.

ANALYSIS

The court here spoke in terms of hearsay but did not identify which exception it was invoking to get by the hearsay problem. At least two are possible. These are present sense impressions and the mental state exceptions. Which one the court applied here was unclear.

Quicknotes

PRESENT SENSE IMPRESSION A statement describing or explaining an event or condition, made while or immediately after the declarant perceived it. Fed. R. Evid 803(1). It is an exception to the hearsay rule.

PROBATIVE Tending to establish proof.

RELEVANT EVIDENCE Evidence having any tendency to prove or disprove a disputed fact.

STATE-OF-MIND EXCEPTION An exception to the hearsay rule; an out-of-court declaration of an existing motive is admissible, even when the declarant cannot testify in person.

United States v. Arnold

Federal government (P) v. Convicted murderer (D)

486 F.3d 177 (6th Cir. 2007)

NATURE OF CASE: Appeal from a conviction for being a felon in possession of a firearm.

FACT SUMMARY: Shortly after a man threatened a woman with a handgun, she told the police about the incident. She did not testify at trial, but her out-of-court statements to the police were admitted into evidence at the man's trial.

RULE OF LAW
Out-of-court statements prompted by a startling event can qualify as excited utterances even if the evidence fails to show precisely how much time elapsed between the event and the statements.

FACTS: An excited Tamica Gordon told a 911 operator that previously convicted murderer Joseph Arnold (D) had pulled a handgun on her, cocked it, and threatened to kill her. Officers responded to the call, and Arnold (D) returned to the house shortly thereafter. At that point, Gordon again became excited, repeatedly identifying Arnold (D) for the officers as "the guy that pulled the gun on me." A search of the car in which Arnold (D) arrived revealed a handgun that fit the description of the gun that Gordon claimed Arnold (D) had used to threaten her. A grand jury returned an indictment charging Arnold (D) with being a felon in possession of a firearm. Gordon did not testify at Arnold's (D) trial, but her statements to the 911 operator and to the officers were admitted under the "excited utterance" exception to the hearsay rule. Arnold (D) was convicted, and he appealed, challenging the admission of Gordon's out-of-court statements.

ISSUE: Can out-of-court statements prompted by a startling event qualify as excited utterances even if the evidence fails to show precisely how much time elapsed between the event and the statements?

HOLDING AND DECISION: (Sutton, J.) Yes. Out-of-court statements prompted by a startling event can qualify as excited utterances even if the evidence fails to show precisely how much time elapsed between the event and the statements. Federal Rule of Evidence 803(2) permits a court to admit out-of-court statements for the truth of the matter asserted if a startling event prompted the statements and the declarant was still "under the stress of excitement" when making the statements. The party offering such evidence must make three showings: (1) a sufficiently startling event, (2) a lack of time in which the declarant could have "contrived or misrepresented" before making the statements, and (3) the continuing existence of excitement from the startling event during the making of the statements. [This case involves three sets of out-of-court statements: those Gordon made in the 911 call, those she made to the officers before Arnold (D) returned, and those she made to the officers after Arnold (D) returned.] The first and third factors are satisfied with respect to the 911 call: being threatened with a gun by a convicted murderer is a startling event, and Gordon clearly remained excited during the call. The trial court specifically found that Gordon said, "[H]e's fixing to shoot me." The immediacy between the event and the utterance, [based on the use of the present progressive form in Gordon's verb,] thus shows that Gordon's statements in the call occurred before she had time to contrive or misrepresent. The Government's (P) failure to show precisely how much time elapsed between the event and these statements is irrelevant because such a showing is not necessary under the law of this circuit. Further, Gordon's "crying" and "hysterical" condition when the officers arrived shows that she was still excited in response to the same startling event that prompted her 911 call. Also, the length of time between the call and the officers' arrival—estimated at 5 to 21 minutes—was not enough to give Gordon an opportunity to fabricate. Nor was the length of time between the event and Arnold's (D) arrival—estimated at 30 seconds to 5 minutes after the officers' arrival—enough to provide an opportunity to contrive or misrepresent. Accordingly, the trial court correctly admitted all of Gordon's out-of-court statements. Affirmed.

DISSENT: (Moore, J.) Gordon's out-of-court statements do not qualify as excited utterances, and they therefore should have been excluded. No evidence suggests how much time elapsed between the event and the 911 call. The evidence does not support a reasonable inference, one way or the other, on whether Gordon used the present or past tense in her statement about Arnold (D) "fixing to shoot" her. Gordon herself further undermined the reliability of her statement to the 911 operator by prefacing it with the words "I guess." The majority circumvents these evidentiary deficiencies by impermissibly collapsing the second inquiry into the third—by using Gordon's excited state also as proof that insufficient time for contrivance or misrepresentation had elapsed. Furthermore, both of the other two sets of statements also fail to qualify as excited utterances.

Continued on next page.

ANALYSIS

Like all other exceptions to the hearsay rule, the excited-utterance exception is based on assumption that independent indicia of reliability can render a hearsay statement sufficiently reliable for courts to tolerate the hearsay. Gordon's out-of-court statements in *Arnold*—which the Government (P) offered against Arnold (D) to prove that he had, in fact, possessed a firearm when he was a convicted felon—show that fundamental principle in action. Her statements were made in such a frantic emotional state that the risk of dishonesty is so diminished that the statements can be admitted as reliable evidence that the described events did indeed occur.

Quicknotes

EXCITED UTTERANCE An exception to the hearsay rule for a statement relating to a startling event or condition, made while the declarant was under the stress of excitement that it caused. Fed. R. Evid. 803(2).

HEARSAY RULE Rule that an out-of-court statement made by a person other than the witness testifying at trial and that is offered in order to prove the truth of the matter asserted is inadmissible.

Mutual Life Insurance Co. v. Hillmon

Insurance company (D) v. Wife of decedent (P)

145 U.S. 285 (1892)

NATURE OF CASE: Appeal from judgment enforcing life-insurance policies.

FACT SUMMARY: Mutual Life Insurance Co. (D) contended that letters written by the person it claimed was the actual decedent and indicating that person's intention to accompany Hillmon, the purported decedent and insured, were relevant and admissible to prove a conspiracy theory that Hillmon had not died and therefore his wife was not entitled to the insurance proceeds.

RULE OF LAW

Contemporaneous oral or written declarations that demonstrate a party's intent are admissible when that party's intentions are a material fact at issue in the case.

FACTS: Mrs. Hillmon (P) sued to collect the proceeds of three separate life insurance policies. She contended that her husband, a cowboy and adventurer, had died in March 1879, when he was accidentally shot by his companion, Brown. The insurance companies rejected the claim based on declarations made by Brown that Mr. Hillmon and he had in fact murdered a Mr. Walters, whom they met along the way, and attempted to pass Walters's body off as Hillmon's in an attempt to defraud the insurance companies. In support of this defense, Mutual Life Insurance Co. (Mutual) (D) attempted to admit into evidence certain letters written by Walters to different members of his family, which placed him in geographic proximity to Mr. Hillmon and Brown and mentioned that Walters would be accompanying Mr. Hillmon. Mrs. Hillmon (P) objected to the admission of such letters into evidence as inadmissible hearsay. The letters were ruled inadmissible, and a verdict for Mrs. Hillmon (P) was entered. Mutual (D) and the other carriers appealed.

ISSUE: Are contemporaneous oral or written declarations that demonstrate a party's intent admissible when that party's intentions are a material fact at issue in the case?

HOLDING AND DECISION: (Gray, J.) Yes. Contemporaneous oral or written declarations that demonstrate a party's intent are admissible when that party's intentions are a material fact at issue in the case. The letters in question were competent evidence that shortly before the time when Walters went away, he had the intention of going, and of going with Mr. Hillmon, and that he was in fact the person whose body was offered as the decedent. Thus, the mental feelings of Walters were material in the case with regard to his intention to accompany Mr. Hillmon. There was no other way of showing those intentions due to Walters's death; however, they were just as competent as if he had testified to them himself. The letters can be regarded as verbal acts and are as competent as any other testimony due to their relevance. Whether or not they are true or false is a question for the jury. As a result, the two letters involved were competent evidence of Walters's intention at the time of writing them, which was a material fact bearing upon the question in controversy. Reversed and remanded.

ANALYSIS

It is clear that the letters written in this case could have been excluded under the hearsay rule. They were clearly out-of-court statements offered for their truth. However, they fell within the subsequent-conduct exception recognized by some jurisdictions. The use of the letters was not allowed as independent evidence of Walters's death by Mr. Hillmon. However, they were competent as corroborating evidence. The case does not specifically elucidate the other evidence presented by the carriers to determine that Walters was, in fact, the decedent, but it is made clear by the court that the letters were merely corroborating evidence and if offered on their own might not have been considered competent. This is a relatively broad application of an exception to the hearsay rule. Impacting upon this are the indices of the reliability inherent in the letters. There would not appear to have been any alternative motive behind the creation of such letters, and, therefore, the court made a determination that the reliability was high enough to allow them into evidence.

Quicknotes

HEARSAY RULE Rule that an out-of-court statement made by a person other than the witness testifying at trial and that is offered in order to prove the truth of the matter asserted is inadmissible.

MATERIAL ISSUE OF FACT An issue or dispute regarding a fact that is legally relevant to a claim or cause of action that will, as a matter of substantive law, make a difference to the outcome reached in a given case. Frequently stated as "issue of material fact."

United States v. Pheaster

Federal government (P) v. Criminals (D)

544 F.2d 353 (9th Cir. 1976), *cert. denied,* 429 U.S. 1099 (1979)

NATURE OF CASE: Appeal from various criminal convictions including conspiracy.

FACT SUMMARY: Inciso (D) claimed that it was error for the trial court to have admitted into evidence statements of intention made by the party that he and others, including Pheaster (D), had allegedly conspired to kidnap.

RULE OF LAW

Under the *Hillmon* doctrine, the state-of-mind exception to the hearsay rule allows the admission of a statement from the declarant of the declarant's intent to do something with another individual, allowing the trier of fact to infer that the declarant followed through with his or her intention to commit the stated act.

FACTS: Inciso (D), Pheaster (D), and others were allegedly part of a plot to kidnap and hold for ransom Larry Adell, the 16-year-old son of a Palm Springs multimillionaire. Larry disappeared forever after leaving his friends at a table at a local restaurant known as Sambo's North, telling them he was going to meet Angelo and he'd be right back. Earlier that day, he had told his girlfriend that he was going to meet Angelo at Sambo's North at 9:30 that night to pick up a pound of marijuana Angelo had promised him for free. Larry's girlfriend had been with Larry another time when he had met a man named Angelo. At trial Larry's girlfriend identified Inciso (D) as that man. Inciso (D) objected to the introduction of this testimony concerning the statements Larry made to others. The Government (P) insisted it was admissible under the *Hillmon* doctrine, *Mutual Life Insurance Co. v. Hillmon*, 145 U.S. 285 (1892), to show Larry's state of mind and thus prove by inference that he acted in accordance with his intention to meet Angelo and did meet him.

ISSUE: Under the *Hillmon* doctrine, does the state-of-mind exception to the hearsay rule allow the admission of a statement from the declarant of the declarant's intent to do something with another individual, allowing the trier of fact to infer that the declarant followed through with his or her intention to commit the stated act?

HOLDING AND DECISION: (Renfrew, J.) Yes. Under the *Hillmon* doctrine, the state-of-mind exception to the hearsay rule allows the admission of a statement from the declarant of the declarant's intent to do something with another individual, allowing the trier of fact to infer that the declarant followed through with his or her intention to commit the stated act. The *Hillmon* doctrine is a particular species of the "state-of-mind" exception to the general rule that hearsay evidence is inadmissible. Under the *Hillmon* doctrine, which takes its name from the famous United States Supreme Court decision in *Mutual Life Insurance Co. v. Hillmon*, 145 U.S. 285 (1892), the state of mind of the declarant is used inferentially to prove other matters that are in issue. It does not require that the state of mind of the declarant be an actual issue in the case. Stated simply, the doctrine provides that when the performance of a particular act by an individual is an issue in a case, the individual's intention (state of mind) to perform that act may be shown. From that intention, the trier of fact may draw the inference that the person carried out his or her intention and performed the act. Within this conceptual framework, hearsay evidence of statements by the person that tend to show the person's intention is deemed admissible under the state-of-mind exception. Inciso's (D) objection concerns application of this doctrine to situations in which the declarant has stated his or her intention to do something with another person, and the issue is whether he or she did so. When hearsay evidence concerns the declarant's statement of the declarant's intention to do something with another person, the *Hillmon* doctrine requires that the trier of fact infer from the state of mind of the declarant the probability of a particular act not only by the declarant but also by the other person. Several objections can be raised against a doctrine that would allow such an inference to be made. First, it is an unreliable inference. More importantly, however, such an inference is inconsistent with the state-of-mind exception. Part of the statement that is admitted has nothing to do with the declarant's state of mind. If Larry's friends had testified that he said, "Angelo is going to be in the parking lot of Sambo's North tonight with a pound of grass," no state-of-mind exception or any other exception to the hearsay rule would be available. Yet, this is in effect at least half of what the testimony did attribute to Larry. Despite the theoretical awkwardness associated with the application of the *Hillmon* doctrine to facts such as those in this case, the authority in favor of such an application is impressive and must be followed. Therefore, although this court recognizes the force of the objection to the application of the *Hillmon* doctrine in the instant case, it cannot conclude that the district court erred in permitting the testimony concerning Larry Adell's statements. Affirmed.

Continued on next page.

ANALYSIS

Although the new Federal Rules of Evidence were not in force when this case came to trial, both the Advisory Committee on the Proposed Rules and the House Committee on the Judiciary specifically addressed the *Hillmon* doctrine in making statements concerning Rule 803(3), which codifies the state-of-mind exception to the hearsay rule but does not provide a direct statement of the *Hillmon* doctrine. The language the House Committee used indicates that both bodies perceived the then-prevailing common-law view to be that the *Hillmon* doctrine could be applied in cases where the hearsay statement of intent by a declarant was admitted to prove the declarant did something with another person. However, the Notes of the House Committee stated its intention that the Rule be construed to limit the *Hillmon* doctrine "so as to render statements of intent by a declarant admissible only to prove the declarant's future conduct, not the future conduct of another person." This is contrary to the view that the Advisory Committee obviously had of the effect of Rule 803(3) on the *Hillmon* doctrine. It stated, "(t)he rule of *Mutual Life Ins. Co. v. Hillmon*, 145 U.S. 285 (1892), . . . allowing evidence of intention as tending to prove the doing of the act intended is, of course, left undisturbed." Note to Paragraph (3), 28 U.S.C.A. at 585.

Quicknotes

HEARSAY RULE Rule that an out-of-court statement made by a person other than the witness testifying at trial and that is offered in order to prove the truth of the matter asserted is inadmissible.

PRESENT STATE-OF-MIND EXCEPTION An exception to the hearsay rule for statements made by an unavailable declarant pertaining to a present motive for his or her conduct.

Blake v. State

Stepfather (D) v. State (P)

Wyo. Sup. Ct., 933 P.2d 474 (1997)

NATURE OF CASE: Appeal from conviction of second-degree sexual assault.

FACT SUMMARY: Blake (D) appealed from his conviction of two counts of second-degree sexual assault of his 16-year-old stepdaughter.

RULE OF LAW

A statement by a child victim to a medical professional is admissible in situations involving physical or sexual abuse of the child.

FACTS: An investigator from the Department of Family Services (DFS) and an officer from the sheriff's office interviewed the victim, a 16-year-old girl, at the local high school in response to a report of sexual abuse. After the interview she was transferred to the hospital emergency room for an examination, during which she told the doctor she had been forcibly subjected to sexual intercourse by her stepfather, Blake (D), several times. The victim was not called to the stand at trial. Instead, the State (P) relied upon Blake's (D) typed confession, and the testimony of the doctor, the DFS investigator, and the officer. The jury convicted Blake (D) of two counts of second-degree sexual assault and Blake (D) appealed.

ISSUE: Is a statement by a child victim to a medical professional admissible in situations involving physical or sexual abuse of the child?

HOLDING AND DECISION: (Lehman, J.) Yes. A statement by a child victim to a medical professional is admissible in situations involving physical or sexual abuse of the child. In order to admit statements of identity, a two-part test must be satisfied in order to establish the proper foundation under *United States v. Renville*, 779 F.2d 430 (8th Cir. 1985). First the declarant's motive in making the statement must be consistent with the purposes of promoting treatment or diagnosis. Second, the content of the statement must be reasonably relied upon by the physician in rendering the treatment or making the diagnosis. Here the State (P) satisfied the *Renville* test and laid the proper foundation. The doctor examined the victim as a result of allegations of sexual abuse. In such sexual assault cases the doctor is required to take a history of the patient regarding what happened in order to ascertain the patient's emotional state and to properly collect specimens and render proper medical treatment. Blake (D) argued that this case was distinguishable since the victim was 17 years old at the time of trial and her statements lacked the credibility of a younger victim. This argument is without merit. The child's age is a factor to be considered in determining the weight of the evidence, not in its admissibility. Blake (D) had an opportunity to attack the victim's credibility and failed to do so. Affirmed.

ANALYSIS

The rule is that statements regarding fault or identity are generally not admissible at trial. The court noted that the statutory exception for statements of child victims to treating physicians was created in order to accommodate for the unique problem of child abuse and to provide proper treatment and diagnosis for such victims.

Quicknotes

CHILD ABUSE Conduct harmful to a child's physical or mental health.

Ohio v. Scott

State (P) v. Convicted shooter (D)

Ohio Sup. Ct., 285 N.E.2d 344 (1972)

NATURE OF CASE: Appeal from criminal convictions.

FACT SUMMARY: Scott (D) objected to the introduction at his criminal trial of a witness's prior written statement to the police as a record of past recollection.

RULE OF LAW

The prior recorded statement of a witness in a criminal trial can be admitted under the hearsay exception for records of "past recollection recorded" without violating the defendant's Sixth Amendment right of confrontation.

FACTS: Scott (D) was convicted of shooting at Williard Lee with intent to kill, wound, or maim, and for shooting at two police officers. On appeal, Scott (D) argued that the trial court had acted improperly in admitting into evidence the statement of a witness who testified that her memory was better at the time she gave the written and signed statement to the police than it was at the time of trial. Scott (D) maintained the rule of "past recollection recorded" had not been recognized in Ohio and that employing it in a criminal case deprived the defendant of his or her Sixth Amendment right of confrontation, including the opportunity of cross-examination. The appellate court affirmed the conviction, and Scott (D) took his arguments to the Ohio Supreme Court.

ISSUE: Can the prior recorded statement of a witness in a criminal trial be admitted under the hearsay exception for records of "past recollection recorded" without violating the defendant's Sixth Amendment right of confrontation?

HOLDING AND DECISION: (Leach, J.) Yes. The prior recorded statement of a witness in a criminal trial can be admitted under the hearsay exception for records of "past recollection recorded" without violating the defendant's Sixth Amendment right of confrontation. So long as the declarant is testifying as a witness, the defendant has the opportunity to conduct a full and effective cross-examination at the time of trial. In this case, the recorded statement consisted of facts of which the witness had firsthand knowledge; it was the original memorandum made near the time of the event while the witness had a clear and accurate memory of it; the witness lacked a present recollection of the exact words Scott (D) had used; and the witness stated that the memorandum was accurate. Thus, all conditions for admissibility were met. Affirmed.

DISSENT: (Corrigan, J.) Aside from the danger that a jury will place too much weight on a written statement, the witness did not testify that she had no present memory of the events recorded therein.

ANALYSIS

Under the traditional approach, such records of past recollection would not be admissible if examining them could refresh the witness's recollection. Courts are split as to whether any recollection at all is sufficient or whether it must be sufficient to enable the witness to testify fully and accurately, a standard that is gaining in popularity.

Quicknotes

CROSS-EXAMINATION The interrogation of a witness by an adverse party either to further inquire as to the subject matter of the direct examination or to call into question the witness's credibility.

PAST RECOLLECTION RECORDED An exception to the hearsay rule for statements contained in a document as to which the witness no longer has recollection.

RIGHT TO CONFRONT WITNESSES A provision in the Sixth Amendment to the U.S. Constitution that an accused in a criminal action has the right to confront the witnesses against him, including the right to attend the trial and to cross-examine witnesses called on behalf of the prosecution.

Petrocelli v. Gallison

Patient (P) v. Surgeon (D)

679 F.2d 286 (1st Cir. 1982)

NATURE OF CASE: Appeal of denial of damages for medical malpractice.

FACT SUMMARY: A trial court excluded from evidence a passage from a hospital record because the source of the information contained therein was uncertain.

RULE OF LAW

For a portion of a business record to be admissible, the source of the information contained therein must be known.

FACTS: Gallison (D) operated on Petrocelli (P) for a hernia. Petrocelli (P) was afforded no pain relief, and several months later a Dr. Schwartz performed a second procedure, which was also unsuccessful. A third operation proved necessary. Petrocelli (P) sued Gallison (D) for malpractice. An important issue was whether Gallison (D) had inadvertently severed a certain nerve. At trial, Petrocelli (P) attempted to introduce a passage from the operative report related to the second procedure that indicated that the nerve had, in fact, been severed in the original procedure. The source of this information was unknown. The trial court excluded the report. The jury rendered a defense verdict, and Petrocelli (P) appealed.

ISSUE: For a portion of a business record to be admissible, must the source of the information contained therein be known?

HOLDING AND DECISION: (Campbell, J.) Yes. For a portion of a business record to be admissible, the source of the information contained therein must be known. For the business-record exception to the hearsay rule to be applicable, it must be demonstrable that the information contained in the record be transmitted by a person with knowledge of the information and be done in the usual course of business. When a record is completely devoid of any indication as to the source of the information, it cannot be shown that the information therein was, in fact, transmitted by a knowledgeable person. Here, no indication of the source of the information can be found. It is quite likely that the information can be found. It is quite likely that the information came from Petrocelli (P) himself, an individual unqualified to make such an assertion. It was within the trial court's discretion to exclude the evidence. Affirmed.

ANALYSIS

It would have seemed fairly certain that the evidence came from either the doctors or the Petrocellis (P). Had it come from the doctors, the hearsay exception at issue would have been available. The court discussed whether this issue should have gone to the jury. It concluded that it should not have, as this was within the province of the court under Fed. R. Evid. 104(a).

Quicknotes

BUSINESS RECORDS EXCEPTION Exception to the hearsay rule for records made in the ordinary course of business.

FED. R. EVID. 104 Permits a court to consider all nonprivileged matters, whether independently admissible or not, when determining preliminary issues of admissibility.

Norcon, Inc. v. Kotowski

Employer (D) v. Employee (P)

Alaska Sup. Ct., 971 P.2d 158 (1999)

NATURE OF CASE: Sexual harassment suit.

FACT SUMMARY: Norcon, Inc. (D) appealed from a jury verdict in favor of Kotowski (P) in a sexual-harassment suit on the basis that the lower court improperly admitted a three-page, handwritten memo under the official business-records exception to the hearsay rule.

RULE OF LAW

Information that is otherwise hearsay may be admissible under the ordinary business-records exception, so long as all the persons furnishing the information to be recorded are acting in the regular course of business.

FACTS: Kotowski (P) worked on the cleanup of the Exxon Valdez oil spill. Veco, the general contractor, and Norcon, Inc. (D), a subcontractor, had strict rules against alcohol consumption by persons working on the project or living in company housing. Kotowski (P) told Savell, the Exxon executive in charge, that Posehn, Norcon, Inc.'s (D) foreman, was sexually harassing her, that he had invited her to his room that evening, and that he expected alcohol to be consumed. Savell gave her a tape recorder and a note stating she had been assigned to help gather information related to drug and/or alcohol abuse, and that she had amnesty from prosecution and termination of her employment. Kotowski (P) was later questioned regarding the party at Posehn's room. Both Posehn and Kotowski (P) were fired. The jury found Norcon, Inc. (D) liable for sexual harassment and negligent infliction of emotional distress. Kotowski (P) offered into evidence a three-page, handwritten memo summarizing information gathered by a security investigator regarding Posehn. The memo stated that Posehn had many female visitors in his room and that he used the consumption of alcoholic beverages as a "springboard" for sexual activity with female subordinates. The memo also stated that Posehn would do favors for female employees in exchange for sexual activity. Norcon, Inc. (D) objected to the admission of the memo on the basis that it was inadmissible hearsay. Kotowski (P) argued that the memo was admissible under the official business-records exception. Norcon, Inc. (D) contested that argument on the basis that the report contained hearsay statements of others. The superior court admitted the memo under the exception. Norcon, Inc. (D) appealed.

ISSUE: May information that is otherwise hearsay be admissible under the ordinary business-records exception, so long as all the persons furnishing the information to be recorded are acting in the regular course of business?

HOLDING AND DECISION: (Matthews, J.) Yes. Information that is otherwise hearsay may be admissible under the ordinary business-records exception, so long as all the persons furnishing the information to be recorded are acting in the regular course of business. Norcon, Inc. (D) objected to the memo here on the basis that the memo consisted of double and triple hearsay of the informants who provided the information contained in the memo. Norcon, Inc. (D) further argued that even if the memo was prepared in the regular course of business, there was no evidence the informants were acting in the regular course of their business. Kotowski (P) argued that the informants had business reasons, as employees of Norcon, Inc. (D), to provide accurate and true statements. Moreover, Kotowski (P) argued such statements should not be treated as hearsay but rather as admissions of a party-opponent. This argument has merit. The lower court did not err by admitting the memo.

ANALYSIS

The official business-records exception to the hearsay rule is satisfied if all of the following requirements are met: (1) the record is one that is regularly kept in the course of regular business; (2) the source of the information is a person who has personal knowledge of the information stated therein; (3) the information was collected and recorded at a time contemporaneous with the activity observed; and (4) proper foundation is laid by the custodian of the records or another similarly qualified witness.

Quicknotes

BUSINESS RECORD A record made as part of routine procedure; admissible as an exception to the hearsay rule.

BUSINESS RECORDS EXCEPTION Exception to the hearsay rule for records made in the ordinary course of business.

Baker v. Elcona Homes Corp.

Automobile passenger (P) v. Employee truck driver (D)

588 F.2d 551 (6th Cir. 1978), *cert. denied*, 441 U.S. 933 (1979)

NATURE OF CASE: Action for damages for negligence.

FACT SUMMARY: Baker (P), who sued to recover damages for a car accident with a truck driven by an Elcona Homes Corp. (Elcona) (D) employee, objected to the introduction of a police accident report into evidence.

RULE OF LAW

Factual findings in public police reports of an investigation made pursuant to authority granted by law are admissible, unless the party challenging the report can demonstrate that the circumstances surrounding the report lack trustworthiness.

FACTS: A police accident report was put into evidence when Baker (P) brought a negligence suit to recover damages from Elcona Homes Corp. (Elcona) (D) for an accident between one of its truck drivers and the car in which she was riding. The reports contained the officer's opinion that the car had failed to yield the right of way and stated it had "apparently" entered the intersection against a red light. It also contained a statement the truck driver gave to the officer. On appeal from a verdict for Elcona (D), Baker (P) argued these were not the type of "factual findings" admissible under the exception to the hearsay rule for official written statements in Fed. R. Evid. 803(8).

ISSUE: Are factual findings in public police records of an investigation made pursuant to authority granted by law admissible, unless the party challenging the report can demonstrate that the circumstances surrounding the report lack trustworthiness?

HOLDING AND DECISION: (Engel, J.) Yes. Factual findings in public police reports of an investigation made pursuant to authority granted are admissible, unless the party challenging the report can demonstrate that the circumstances surrounding the report lack trustworthiness. Fed. R. Evid. 803(8) provides that public records can be admitted into evidence under an exception to the hearsay rule. It specifically mentions that the factual findings therein (a term that includes evaluations and opinions) are admissible in civil proceedings and against the government in criminal proceedings unless the sources of information or their circumstances indicate lack of trustworthiness. The four factors to be considered in making that determination are: (1) the timeliness of the investigation; (2) the special skill of or experience of the official; (3) whether a hearing was held on the level at which the investigation was conducted; and (4) possible motivational problems. In this case, they point to the trustworthiness of the objected-to opinions and evaluations in the police report. As to the presence of a statement by the truck driver, it is not hearsay because it is a statement consistent with his testimony and offered to rebut the charge that he recently fabricated his story. Admission of the evidence objected to was entirely proper. Affirmed.

ANALYSIS

The common-law requirement that the official making the report have firsthand knowledge of those things he or she records prevented expansion of the official-written-statements exception to the hearsay rule. However, the Federal Rules of Evidence adopted the less stringent rule of admissibility cited in this case. The Uniform Rules of Evidence have opted for an even broader rule.

Quicknotes

FED. R. EVID. 803 Rule setting forth certain exceptions to the hearsay rule, including present sense impressions, excited utterances, present state of mind, statements for medical diagnosis, past recollection recorded, etc.

PUBLIC-RECORDS EXCEPTION Exception to the hearsay rule for the introduction of public records and reports made within the scope of a public employee's official duties, made close to the time of the event and with other indicia of trustworthiness.

Barber v. Page

Convicted robber (D) v. Government (P)

390 U.S. 719 (1968)

NATURE OF CASE: Appeal from a conviction for armed robbery.

FACT SUMMARY: Barber (D) contended the trial court erred in admitting into evidence prior testimony of a co-defendant inculpating him of the crime over his objections, which deprived him of his right to confrontation.

RULE OF LAW

A witness is not unavailable for purposes of the prior-testimony exception to the confrontation requirement unless the prosecutorial authorities have made a good-faith effort to obtain the witness's presence at trial.

FACTS: Barber (D) and Woods were jointly charged with armed robbery. At the preliminary hearing both were represented by the same counsel. Woods agreed to waive his privilege against self-incrimination, and his counsel withdrew as his attorney. That counsel, however, continued to represent Barber (D). Woods made incriminating statements against himself and Barber (D) at the preliminary hearing. Barber's (D) counsel did not cross-examine Woods at the preliminary hearing; however, an attorney for another co-defendant did. At the time of trial, Woods was incarcerated in a federal penitentiary outside the jurisdiction of the court. The prosecution attempted to admit into evidence the transcript of the preliminary hearing that recorded Woods's testimony, arguing that he was unavailable to testify because he was outside the jurisdiction. The prosecution represented to the court that they had not actually inquired of federal authorities whether or not Woods could have been brought to the jurisdiction, explaining that because such a decision on the part of federal authorities would have been discretionary, they did not feel that they were required to actually attempt to bring Woods to the court. Barber (D) objected to the admission of such evidence on the basis that it deprived him of his right to confrontation. The court allowed the evidence, and Barber (D) was convicted. He sought federal habeas corpus relief, which was denied. The United States Supreme Court granted certiorari.

ISSUE: Is a witness unavailable for purposes of the prior-testimony exception to the confrontation requirement only if the prosecutorial authorities have made a good-faith effort to obtain the witness's presence at trial?

HOLDING AND DECISION: (Marshall, J.) Yes. A witness is not unavailable for purposes of the prior-testimony exception to the confrontation requirement unless the prosecutorial authorities have made a good-faith effort to obtain the witness's presence at trial. Because of the clearly increased cooperation between the federal and state governments, it was unconscionable for the prosecutorial authorities to make no attempt to bring Woods to Barber's (D) trial. Their failure to exercise even minimal efforts to bring the witness to the trial eliminated the necessity requirement of using the preliminary hearing transcript. It is this necessity requirement that underlies the rationale for the exception to the Confrontation Clause upon which the Government (P) relied. Because this necessity was absent, the use of the preliminary hearing transcript was an error, and the conviction must be overturned. Reversed and remanded.

ANALYSIS

The Government (P) attempted to argue that Barber (D) had an opportunity to cross-examine Woods at the preliminary hearing, and his failure to do so waived his ability to assert the confrontation defense. However, the Court recognized that there are different motivations at a preliminary hearing than there are at trial. The purpose of the preliminary hearing is merely to establish whether or not there is probable cause to bind the defendant over for trial. Thus, whether or not the decision is to cross-examine or not is made upon different grounds than if the witness were present at trial. Depriving a defendant of his or her right to cross-examine, merely because he or she failed to do so at the preliminary hearing, would clearly infringe upon his or her rights unfairly. The Court concludes that while actual unavailability need not be shown, at least a good-faith effort must be made to produce the actual witness at trial.

Quicknotes

CONFRONTATION CLAUSE A provision in the Sixth Amendment to the U.S. Constitution that an accused in a criminal action has the right to confront the witnesses against him or her, including the right to attend the trial and to cross-examine witnesses called on behalf of the prosecution.

CROSS-EXAMINE Interrogate a witness of an adverse party either to further inquire as to the subject matter

Continued on next page.

of the direct examination or to call into question the witness's credibility.

GOOD FAITH An honest intention to abstain from taking advantage of another.

PRIOR-TESTIMONY EXCEPTION Exception to the hearsay rule for testimony given in a prior proceeding that may be offered in a later proceeding under certain circumstances.

Lloyd v. American Export Lines, Inc.

Seaman (P) v. Shipping company (D)

580 F.2d 1179 (3d Cir.), *cert. denied*, 439 U.S. 969 (1978)

NATURE OF CASE: Counterclaim for damages for negligence and unseaworthiness.

FACT SUMMARY: In defending against a counterclaim brought by Alvarez (D), American Export Lines, Inc. (Export) (D) sought to introduce into evidence testimony that Lloyd (P) (who was unavailable) had given at a Coast Guard hearing regarding the fight between himself and Alvarez (D) aboard one of Export's (D) ships.

RULE OF LAW

The prior testimony of an unavailable witness is admissible under Fed. R. Evid. 804(b)(1) if the party against whom it is offered or a "predecessor in interest" had the "opportunity and similar motive to develop the testimony by direct, cross-, or redirect examination."

FACTS: There was a fight between two crew members, Lloyd (P) and Alvarez (D), aboard an American Export Lines, Inc. (Export) (D) ship. Lloyd (P) sued Export (D), alleging negligence and unseaworthiness. Export (D) joined Alvarez (D) as a third-party defendant, and Alvarez (D) then counterclaimed against Export (D), alleging negligence and unseaworthiness—based on Export's (D) supposed failure to use reasonable precautions to safeguard him from one it knew to have dangerous propensities, i.e., Lloyd (P). Lloyd's (P) case was dismissed when he repeatedly failed to show up for pretrial depositions and when his case was called for trial. Alvarez (D) proceeded with his counterclaim, testifying to his version of the fight that had occurred between himself and Lloyd (P). The trial court did not permit Export (D) to introduce into evidence Lloyd's (P) prior testimony at a Coast Guard hearing that had been held to determine whether his merchant mariner's document should have been suspended or revoked on the basis of charges of misconduct brought against him for the fight with Alvarez (D). That testimony contained Lloyd's (P) quite different account of the fight that had occurred. At that hearing, both Lloyd (P) and Alvarez (D) were represented by counsel and testified under oath. On appeal, Export (D) argued that the trial court had erred in ruling that this prior testimony was not admissible under Fed. R. Evid. 804(b)(1), which renders admissible the prior testimony of an unavailable witness if the party against whom it is offered or a "predecessor in interest" had the "opportunity and similar motive to develop the testimony by direct, cross-, or redirect examination."

ISSUE: If a witness is unavailable, does Fed. R. Evid. 804(b)(1) make the witness's prior testimony admissible if the party against whom it is offered or a "predecessor in interest" had the "opportunity and similar motive to develop the testimony by direct, cross-, or redirect examination?"

HOLDING AND DECISION: (Aldisert, J.) Yes. Under Fed. R. Evid. 804(b)(1), the prior testimony of a witness who is "unavailable" is admissible if the party against whom it is offered or a "predecessor in interest" had the "opportunity and similar motive to develop the testimony by direct, cross-, or redirect examination." In this case, it is clear that the proponent of Lloyd's (P) statement was unable to procure his attendance by process or other reasonable means and that he must thus be considered to have been "unavailable." As to whether American Export Lines, Inc. (D) can be considered a "predecessor in interest" of Lloyd (D), that is a more difficult question. Congress did not define that phrase, leaving it up to the courts to interpret it. As originally submitted by the United States Supreme Court, Rule 804(b)(1) would have allowed prior testimony of an unavailable witness to be received in evidence if the party against whom it was offered, or a person with "motive and interest similar," had an opportunity to examine the witness. The change in wording that occurred thereafter to that which is now set forth in Rule 804(b)(1) did not signal a return to the common-law approach to former testimony—which required privity or a common property interest between the parties. With that in mind, this court is satisfied that there was a sufficient community of interest shared by the Coast Guard in its hearing and Alvarez (D) in the subsequent civil trial to satisfy Rule 804(b)(1). The Coast Guard investigating officer attempted to establish at the Coast Guard hearing what Alvarez (D) attempted to establish at the later trial: Lloyd's (P) intoxication, his role as the aggressor, and his prior hostility toward Alvarez (D). While the result sought in the two proceedings differed, the basic interest advanced by both was that of determining culpability and, if appropriate, exacting a penalty for the same condemned behavior thought to have occurred. Under the circumstances, this court is satisfied that there existed sufficient "opportunity and similar motive (for the Coast Guard investigating officer) to develop (Lloyd's) testimony" at the former hearing to justify its admission against Alvarez (D) at the later trial. It is this court's belief that Congress intended that when a party in a former suit had a like motive to cross-examine regarding the same matters as the present party would have and had an adequate opportunity to do so,

Continued on next page.

the testimony thus procured in that former suit is admissible against the present party because the previous party was, in the final analysis, a predecessor in interest to the present party. Reversed and remanded.

CONCURRENCE: (Stern, J.) While I agree with the result, I cannot agree with the analysis. I would hold that the prior testimony is admissible under the catchall exception to the hearsay rule, 804(b)(5), and not under 804(b)(1). Under the majority's approach, it is sufficient that the Coast Guard investigator and Alvarez (D) shared a community of interest, which the majority seems to think means nothing more than similarity of interest or similarity of motive. But similar motive is a separate prerequisite to admissibility under 804(b)(1), and thus the majority's analysis, which reads "predecessor in interest" to mean nothing more than person with "similar motive," eliminates the predecessor-in-interest requirement entirely. It seems clear that the phrase "predecessor in interest" is a term of art having a narrow, substantive-law sense that historically requires it to be defined in terms of a privity relationship. No such relationship existed in this case. While the interests of Alvarez (D) and the Coast Guard may overlap, they do not coincide. The Coast Guard investigating officer was under no duty to advance every arguable issue against Lloyd (P) in vindication of Alvarez's (D) interests. He simply did not represent Alvarez (D).

ANALYSIS

Just precisely when a witness is "unavailable" so that his or her prior testimony may be admissible is a problem that has plagued the courts. While some have held that a witness's loss of memory of the relevant matters does not render him or her "unavailable," the general consensus is that it does; so too does his or her refusal to testify.

Quicknotes

CROSS-EXAMINATION The interrogation of a witness by an adverse party either to further inquire as to the subject matter of the direct examination or to call into question the witness's credibility.

DIRECT EXAMINATION The initial interrogation of a witness, conducted by the party who called the witness.

PRIOR-TESTIMONY EXCEPTION Exception to the hearsay rule for testimony given in a prior proceeding that may be offered in a later proceeding under certain circumstances.

PRIVITY Commonality of rights or interests between parties.

REDIRECT EXAMINATION A second direct examination of a witness; done after cross-examination; ordinarily the scope of questioning is limited to matters covered during cross-examination.

SUBSTANTIVE LAW Law that pertains to the rights and interests of the parties and upon which a cause of action may be based.

Williamson v. United States

Convicted drug offender (D) v. Federal government (P)

512 U.S. 594 (1994)

NATURE OF CASE: Appeal from conviction of possession of cocaine with intent to distribute, conspiracy to possess cocaine with intent to distribute, and traveling interstate to promote the distribution of cocaine.

FACT SUMMARY: Williamson (D) contended that the district court erred in allowing the testimony of a Drug Enforcement Administration agent in court who related arguably self-inculpatory statements made out of court to him by Harris, one of Williamson's (D) employees, regarding the possession and transport of the cocaine.

RULE OF LAW

Fed. R. Evid. 804(b)(3) does not allow admission of non-self-inculpatory statements, even if they are made within a broader narrative that is generally self-inculpatory.

FACTS: Harris, an employee of Williamson (D), was stopped by the police while he was driving. The police, after searching the car, found 19 kilograms of cocaine in the car and arrested Harris. After his arrest, Harris was interviewed by telephone by Drug Enforcement Administration Agent Walton. Harris told Agent Walton that he had gotten the cocaine from a Cuban, that the cocaine belonged to Williamson (D), and that Harris was delivering it to a particular dumpster for pickup. Shortly thereafter, Agent Walton interviewed Harris personally; Harris then told Agent Walton he was transporting the cocaine to Atlanta for Williamson (D); that Williamson (D) was traveling ahead of him in another car at the time of the arrest; and that Williamson (D) had apparently seen the police searching Harris's car and had fled. Harris told Agent Walton that he had initially lied about the source of the cocaine because he was afraid of Williamson (D). Harris implicated himself in his statements to Agent Walton but did not want his story to be recorded and refused to sign a written transcript of the statement. Agent Walton later testified that Harris was not promised any reward for cooperating. Williamson (D) was eventually charged and convicted of various drug-related offenses. When Harris was called to testify at Williamson's (D) trial, he refused to do so. The district court then ruled that, under Fed. R. Evid. 804(b)(3), Agent Walton could relate what Harris told him because Harris's statements were against his own interests. Williamson (D) was convicted, and the court of appeals affirmed. On appeal, Williamson (D) argued that both lower courts erred by allowing Agent Walton to testify regarding Harris's out-of-court statements.

ISSUE: Does Fed. R. Evid. 804(b)(3) allow admission of non-self-inculpatory statements, even if they are made within a broader narrative that is generally self-inculpatory?

HOLDING AND DECISION: (O'Connor, J.) No. Fed. R. Evid. 804(b)(3) does not allow admission of non-self-inculpatory statements, even if they are made within a broader narrative that is generally self-inculpatory. The district court may not just assume, for purposes of the Rule, that a statement is self-inculpatory because it is part of a fuller confession, and this is especially true when the statement implicates someone else. The question under the Rule is always whether the statement was sufficiently against the declarant's penal interest that a reasonable person would not have made the statement unless believing it to be true. This question can only be answered in light of all the surrounding circumstances. In this case, some of Harris's confession would clearly have been admissible under the Rule. For instance, when he said he knew there was cocaine in the car, he forfeited his only defense to the charge of cocaine possession—lack of knowledge. But other parts of his confession, especially those in which he implicated Williamson (D), did little to subject Harris to criminal liability. A reasonable person in Harris's position might think that implicating someone else would decrease his own exposure to criminal liability at sentencing. Nothing in the record shows that the district court or court of appeals inquired whether each of the statements in Harris's confession was truly self-inculpatory. Vacated and remanded to the court of appeals to conduct this inquiry.

CONCURRENCE: (Scalia, J.) A declarant's statement is not magically transformed from a statement against penal interest into one that is inadmissible merely because the declarant names another person or implicates a possible codefendant. The relevant inquiry, however—and one that is not furthered by clouding the waters with manufactured categories such as "collateral neutral" and "collateral self-serving"—must always be whether the particular remark at issue (and not the extended narrative) meets the standard set forth in Fed. R. Eivd. 804(b)(3).

CONCURRENCE: (Ginsburg, J.) An arrested person has "strong incentive to shift blame or downplay his or her own role" in hope of leniency and a shorter

Continued on next page.

sentence. Hence, none of the statements by Harris fit the exception, "even in part." The remand is justified only to let the government argue that admitting the statement was harmless error.

CONCURRENCE: (Kennedy, J.) Fed. R. Evid. 804(b)(3) establishes a hearsay exception for statements against penal, proprietary, pecuniary, and legal interest. The text of the Rule does not tell us whether collateral statements are admissible. The Court resolves this issue by adopting the extreme position that no collateral statements are admissible under the Rule. The Court reaches that conclusion by relying on the "principle behind the Rule" that reasonable people do not make statements against their interest unless they are telling the truth, and reasons that this policy "expressed in the statutory text" simply does not extend to collateral statements. To the contrary, three sources indicate that the Rule allows the admission of some collateral statements: first, the Advisory Committee Note to the Rule establishes that some collateral statements are admissible; second, at common law, collateral statements were admissible, and we can presume that Congress intended the principle and terms used in the Federal Rules of Evidence to be applied as they were at common law; third, absent a textual direction to the contrary, we should assume that Congress intended the penal interest exception for inculpatory statements to have some meaningful effect. The exclusion of collateral statements would cause the exclusion of almost all inculpatory statements.

ANALYSIS

As indicated by the Court in *Williamson*, Fed. R. Evid. 804(b)(3) requires that self-inculpatory statements should be examined in terms of the reasonable person and that the declarant believe the statement to be against interest. In order to analyze whether the declarant truly believes his or her statement was against interest, the identity of the person to whom the statement was made should be considered. Although the situation wherein a declarant makes his or her statement to the authorities is the prime example of a statement against interest, if such a statement was made to a trusted friend (who was expected to keep the information secret), it has not necessarily been held that this eliminates the disserving nature of the statement.

Quicknotes

HEARSAY RULE Rule that an out-of-court statement made by a person other than the witness testifying at trial and that is offered in order to prove the truth of the matter asserted is inadmissible.

INCULPATORY Evidence tending to show a person's guilt in committing a criminal act.

State v. Weaver

State (P) v. Caretaker (D)

Iowa Sup. Ct., 554 N.W.2d 240 (1996)

NATURE OF CASE: Appeal from first-degree murder conviction.

FACT SUMMARY: Weaver (D) appealed from her conviction for first-degree murder of 11-month-old Melissa Mathes on the basis of affidavits of several women regarding statements by the child's mother that she hit her head on a coffee table.

RULE OF LAW

In making a trustworthiness determination, the court must consider the declarant's propensity to tell the truth, whether the alleged statements were made under oath, assurances of the declarant's personal knowledge, the time lapse between the event and the statement concerning the event, and the motivations of the declarant.

FACTS: Weaver (D) was charged with first-degree murder and child endangerment of 11-month-old Melissa Mathes. Weaver (D) picked up Melissa at the Mathes's home and later called 911 to report that the child was not breathing. Melissa died of respiratory arrest the following day. An autopsy revealed old and recent injuries consistent with "shaken baby syndrome." After her conviction Weaver (D) moved for a new trial on the basis of affidavits stating that Melissa's mother had said that Weaver (D) did not hurt the child and that the baby had hit her head on a coffee table at their home prior to being placed in Weaver's (D) care. The motion was denied on the basis that the affidavits contained hearsay and did not fall into any exception to the rule. The court of appeals affirmed, and the Iowa Supreme Court remanded to consider a second motion for a new trial based on three new affidavits of other women regarding statements made by Melissa's mother regarding the baby having hit her head on the coffee table that morning.

ISSUE: In making a trustworthiness determination, what factors must the court consider?

HOLDING AND DECISION: (McGiverin, C.J.) In making a trustworthiness determination, the court must consider the declarant's propensity to tell the truth, whether the alleged statements were made under oath, assurances of the declarant's personal knowledge, the time lapse between the event and the statement concerning the event, and the motivations of the declarant. Additional circumstances to be considered include corroboration, the declarant's reaffirmation or recanting of the statement, the credibility of the witness, and the availability of the declarant for cross-examination. Here the court did not abuse its discretion in ruling the affidavits were admissible hearsay evidence in ruling on the defendant's second motion for a new trial. The only issue on appeal here is the trustworthiness of the affidavits and testimony. The district court's factual findings concluded that here the witnesses were credible; the declarant was available to testify; the statements were made in close proximity to the events; the declarant had firsthand knowledge of the information; the statement was unambiguous, voluntary, and made to more than one person on separate occasions; and the statement was corroborated by medical evidence. Thus, the district court's decision to admit the affidavits was not an abuse of discretion. Affirmed.

ANALYSIS

This case deals with the catchall exceptions, now found in Fed. R. Evid. 807. The catchall exceptions allow the court to admit evidence that otherwise constitutes hearsay if it meets the requirements of trustworthiness. Here the hearsay evidence was admitted under the catchall exception for the purpose of introducing exonerating facts.

Quicknotes

CROSS-EXAMINATION The interrogation of a witness by an adverse party either to further inquire as to the subject matter of the direct examination or to call into question the witness's credibility.

HEARSAY EXCEPTION Out-of-court statement made by a person other than the witness testifying at trial that is offered in order to prove the truth of the matter asserted and is admissible at trial notwithstanding the fact that it is hearsay.

Crawford v. Washington

Criminal defendant (D) v. State (P)

541 U.S. 36 (2004)

NATURE OF CASE: Appeal from a criminal conviction.

FACT SUMMARY: When the prosecution played the tape-recorded statement of a witness against him at trial, which did not afford the opportunity for cross-examination, Crawford (D) argued he was denied the Sixth Amendment's guarantee of confrontation.

RULE OF LAW

Where testimonial statements are at issue, the only indicium of reliability sufficient to satisfy constitutional demands is the one the Constitution actually prescribes: confrontation.

FACTS: Michael Crawford (D) stabbed a man who allegedly tried to rape his wife, Sylvia. At his trial, the prosecution played for the jury Sylvia's tape-recorded statement to the police describing the stabbing, even though Crawford (D) had no opportunity for cross-examination. The jury found Crawford (D) guilty. The Washington Court of Appeals reversed, but the Washington Supreme Court upheld the conviction after determining that Sylvia's statement was reliable. Crawford (D) appealed to the United States Supreme Court, contending that the State of Washington's (P) procedure of playing the tape violated the Sixth Amendment's guarantee that in all criminal prosecutions the accused shall enjoy the right to be confronted with the witnesses against him.

ISSUE: Where testimonial statements are at issue, is confrontation the only indicium of reliability sufficient to satisfy constitutional demands?

HOLDING AND DECISION: (Scalia, J.) Yes. Where testimonial statements are at issue, the only indicium of reliability sufficient to satisfy constitutional demands is confrontation. Here, the state admitted Sylvia's testimonial statement against Crawford (D) despite the fact he had no opportunity to cross-examine her. That alone is sufficient to make out a violation of the Sixth Amendment. This court will not mine the record in search of indicia of reliability. Although where nontestimonial hearsay is at issue, it is wholly consistent with the Framers' design to afford the states flexibility in their development of hearsay law. Where testimonial evidence is at issue, the Sixth Amendment demands what the common law required: unavailability and a prior opportunity for cross-examination. Whatever else the term "testimonial" covers, it applies at a minimum to prior testimony at a preliminary hearing, before a grand jury, or at a former trial, and to police interrogations. These are the modern practices with closest kinship to the abuses at which the Confrontation Clause was directed. The Constitution prescribes the procedure for determining the reliability of testimony in criminal trials, and this Court, no less than the state courts, lacks authority to replace it with one of our own devising. By replacing categorical constitutional guarantees with open-ended balancing tests, we would do violence to the Framers' design. Reversed and remanded.

ANALYSIS

In *Crawford*, the United States Supreme Court makes clear that where testimonial statements are involved in criminal cases, the Framers did not intend to leave the Sixth Amendment's protection to the vagaries of the rules of evidence, much less to amorphous notions of "reliability." Legal authorities and scholars do not acknowledge any general reliability exception to the common-law confrontation rule. In this regard, the *Crawford* decision notes that admitting statements simply because they are deemed reliable by a judge is fundamentally at odds with the right of confrontation. While the Sixth Amendment's ultimate goal is to ensure reliability of evidence, it is a procedural rather than a substantive guarantee. It commands not that evidence be reliable, but that reliability is assessed in a particular manner: by cross-examination.

Quicknotes

CONFRONTATION CLAUSE A provision in the Sixth Amendment to the U.S. Constitution that an accused in a criminal action has the right to confront the witnesses against him or her, including the right to attend the trial and to cross-examine witnesses called on behalf of the prosecution.

CROSS-EXAMINATION The interrogation of a witness by an adverse party either to further inquire as to the subject matter of the direct examination or to call into question the witness's credibility.

Davis v. Washington

Criminal defendant (D) v. State (P)

547 U.S. 813 (2006)

NATURE OF CASE: Appeal of convictions for domestic abuse in two similar cases.

FACT SUMMARY: Police arrested Davis (D) after the woman he assaulted in a domestic dispute called 911. At trial, the court allowed admission of the 911 recording. The woman he allegedly assaulted did not testify. In the companion case, *Hammon v. Indiana*, police spoke with Hammon's wife while Hammon (D) was in another room of the house. Hammon's wife informed the police that Hammon assaulted her. The court allowed the police to testify as to Hammon's wife's statements.

RULE OF LAW

Statements made to police are nontestimonial when circumstances indicate objectively that the primary purpose of the statements is to assist the police with an ongoing emergency, rather than to prove or establish past events to assist in a subsequent criminal prosecution.

FACTS: Police arrested Davis (D) after Michelle McCottry called 911 and identified Davis (D) as her assailant in a domestic dispute. At trial, the 911 call was offered as evidence linking Davis (D) to McCottry's injuries, but McCottry did not testify. Davis (D) argued that presenting the recording without giving him the opportunity to cross-examine McCottry violated his Sixth Amendment right to confront his accuser. The Washington Supreme Court disagreed, holding that the call was not testimonial. In *Hammon v. Indiana*, police responded to a domestic disturbance. While Hammon (D) was in another room, Hammon's wife informed the police that Hammon had knocked her down and struck her twice. At trial, Hammon's wife did not appear, but the court allowed the police officer to testify as to what Hammon's wife stated about the assault.

ISSUE: Are statements made to police nontestimonial when circumstances indicate objectively that the primary purpose of the statements is to assist the police with an ongoing emergency, rather than to prove or establish past events to assist in a subsequent criminal prosecution?

HOLDING AND DECISION: (Scalia, J.) Yes. Statements made to police are nontestimonial when circumstances indicate objectively that the primary purpose of the statements is to assist the police with an ongoing emergency, rather than to prove or establish past events to assist in a subsequent criminal prosecution. McCottry's identification of her attacker to the 911 operator was intended to help the police resolve an ongoing emergency, not to testify to a past crime. Under the circumstances, McCottry was not acting as a witness, and the 911 transcript was not testimony. There is no dispute McCottry made her statements to the 911 operator while the emergency was still occurring. Because her statements were not testimonial, the Sixth Amendment's Confrontation Clause did not require her to appear at trial and be cross-examined. The *Davis* decision is affirmed.

In *Hammon*, there was no emergency. Hammon (D) was in another room attended to by a police officer while Hammon's wife described the alleged assault to another police officer. The inquiry was not about what was happening, rather it was about what had happened. Because there was no emergency, the primary purpose of her statements was not to assist the police with an ongoing emergency, but to establish past events. Hammon's (D) conviction is vacated.

CONCURRENCE AND DISSENT: (Thomas, J.) The emergency standard articulated here is not moored in any of our Confrontation Clause jurisprudence. When police respond to a call, particularly a domestic dispute, their purpose is both to resolve ongoing emergencies and to preserve evidence for later use at trial. It is too difficult to determine a police officer's motive during an informal on-scene investigation. The appropriate analysis is to review the formality of the questioning. Because the statements in neither *Davis* nor *Hammond* were conducted in a formalized, custodial setting, the statements were nontestimonial and could be admitted over any Confrontation Clause objections.

ANALYSIS

The United States Supreme Court heard *Davis v. Washington* and *Hammon v. Indiana* in tandem. Both cases involved the issue unresolved in *Crawford v. Washington*, 541 U.S. 36 (2004), in which the Supreme Court held that testimonial statements in a criminal trial are prohibited by the Confrontation Clause of the Sixth Amendment if the defendant was not able to cross-examine the person who made the statement. Review of the existence of emergency circumstances remains the current standard.

Continued on next page.

Quicknotes

CONFRONTATION CLAUSE A provision in the Sixth Amendment to the U.S. Constitution that an accused in a criminal action has the right to confront the witnesses against him or her, including the right to attend the trial and to cross-examine witnesses called on behalf of the prosecution.

CROSS-EXAMINE Interrogate a witness of an adverse party either to further inquire as to the subject matter of the direct examination or to call into question the witness's credibility.

SIXTH AMENDMENT Provides the right to a speedy and public trial by impartial jury, the right to be informed of the accusation, the right to confront witnesses, and the right to have the assistance of counsel in all criminal prosecutions.

CHAPTER 5

Relevance Revisited

Quick Reference Rules of Law

	PAGE
1. *Tuer v. McDonald.* Subsequent remedial measure evidence is not generally admissible for impeachment purposes if it is merely offered to contradict a defense witness's testimony.	*46*

Tuer v. McDonald

Patient's widow (P) v. Doctor (D)

Md. Ct. App., 701 A.2d 1101 (1997)

NATURE OF CASE: Medical malpractice suit.

FACT SUMMARY: Mary Tuer (P) brought suit against St. Joseph's Hospital (D) and two surgeons alleging medical malpractice based on their failure to readminister Heparin, an anticoagulant, to her husband after his surgery was postponed, allegedly leading to his suffering from cardiac arrest and subsequent death.

RULE OF LAW

Subsequent remedial measure evidence is not generally admissible for impeachment purposes if it is merely offered to contradict a defense witness's testimony.

FACTS: Mary Tuer (P) brought a medical malpractice suit against St. Joseph's Hospital (Hospital) (D) and doctors McDonald (D) and Brawley (D) after her husband, Eugene, died of cardiac arrest while awaiting coronary artery bypass graft surgery (CABG). Eugene was admitted to the Hospital (D) and scheduled for surgery. He was placed on Atenol and Heparin. Following Hospital (D) procedure, the anesthesiologist stopped the Heparin Monday morning so that he would not have an anticoagulant in his system during surgery. Eugene was prepared for surgery but an emergency involving another patient required Eugene's surgery to be postponed. Shortly thereafter Eugene went into cardiac arrest and died the next day. After Eugene's death, the Hospital (D) changed its procedure with respect to discontinuing Heparin for patients with stable angina. Heparin is now continued until the patient is taken into the operating room. The defendants made a motion in limine to exclude reference to the change in procedure. Tuer (P) argued that the evidence was admissible since the change was not a remedial measure because the Hospital (D) claimed the prior procedure was correct and that she was entitled to prove the change to show that continuing Heparin was "feasible." The trial court rejected the first argument but stated that it would admit the evidence if the Hospital (D) denied feasibility.

ISSUE: Is subsequent remedial measure evidence generally admissible for impeachment purposes if it is merely offered to contradict a defense witness's testimony?

HOLDING AND DECISION: (Wilner, J.) No. Subsequent remedial measure evidence is not generally admissible for impeachment purposes if it is merely offered to contradict a defense witness's testimony. Maryland Rule of Evidence 5-407 exempts evidence of subsequent remedial measures when it is offered to prove feasibility, if feasibility has been controverted. This requires the court to determine what is meant by the term feasibility and whether feasibility was in fact controverted. Jurisdictions are divided in construing the feasibility exception. One view is that the term feasibility should be defined narrowly, excluding evidence of subsequent remedial measures unless the defendant specifically argues the measures were not possible under the prevailing circumstances. This view states that feasibility is not controverted (and subsequent remedial evidence not admissible) if a defendant contends the design or practice was chosen due to its perceived advantage over the alternative design or practice; if the defendant claims the instructions or warnings were adequate and additional or different warnings or instructions could not have been given; or if the defendant claims the alternative would not have prevented the type of injury sustained in the present case. The other, more expansive view concludes that "feasible" applies not only to that which is possible but includes that which is capable of being utilized successfully. Here the expert testimony did not suggest that the Heparin could not have been readministered following the postponement of Eugene's surgery; instead, they contend there were no signs of renewed unstable angina. McDonald's (D) statement that the Heparin was not continued because he regarded it as unsafe is equal to a statement that it was unfeasible. This statement suffices to controvert the feasibility of the measure. Affirmed.

ANALYSIS

The exclusion of evidence for subsequent remedial measures is based primarily on public policy reasons. The legislature seeks to encourage businesses and persons to adopt improved procedures or designs. If evidence of such improvements were admissible, the fear is that this evidence would lead to a presumption of negligence or admission of guilt with respect to the prior procedure.

Quicknotes

MOTION IN LIMINE Motion by one party brought prior to trial to exclude the potential introduction of prejudicial evidence.

SUBSEQUENT REMEDIAL MEASURES Actions taken by a defendant to correct the instrumentality that caused an injury; inadmissible to show any liability or culpability on the part of the defendant.

CHAPTER 6

Competency of Witnesses

Quick Reference Rules of Law

United States v. Lightly

Federal government (P) v. Convicted felon (D)

677 F.2d 1027 (4th Cir. 1982)

NATURE OF CASE: Appeal of conviction for assault with intent to commit murder.

FACT SUMMARY: A court did not permit McDuffie to testify at trial because he was legally insane.

RULE OF LAW

Legal insanity alone will not make a witness incompetent to testify.

FACTS: Lightly (D) and McDuffie were involved in an incident in which McKinley was seriously injured by repeated stabbings. They were all inmates in the same prison. Lightly (D) was charged with assault with intent to commit murder. McDuffie was not charged, as he was ruled insane and not competent to stand trial. Lightly (D) maintained he had only tried to break up McDuffie's assault upon McKinley. McDuffie was prepared to testify that this was true. The court did not permit McDuffie to testify because of his insanity. Lightly (D) was convicted, and he appealed.

ISSUE: Will legal insanity alone make a witness incompetent to testify?

HOLDING AND DECISION: (Ervin, J.) No. Legal insanity alone will not make a witness incompetent to testify. Every witness is presumed to be competent to testify, unless it can be shown the witness has no relevant knowledge, cannot recall, or cannot testify truthfully. Legal insanity may indeed result in such a disqualification but does not automatically do so. The trial court should have conducted in camera hearing to make this determination. Reversed and remanded.

ANALYSIS

Probably no area of evidence has changed more from the early common-law rules than competency. Common law contained many disqualifications, such as marriage, mental illness, religious beliefs, and criminal convictions. These have all been removed.

Quicknotes

COMPETENCY Those qualifications necessary for a witness to give testimony at a trial consistent with the requirements of law.

IN CAMERA In private chambers.

United States v. Fowler

Federal government (P) v. Tax protester (D)

605 F.2d 181 (5th Cir. 1979)

NATURE OF CASE: Appeal of conviction for tax evasion.

FACT SUMMARY: Fowler (D), who was charged with tax evasion, was not permitted to testify because he refused to swear to tell the truth.

RULE OF LAW

One may not testify if one refuses to swear to tell the truth.

FACTS: Fowler (D), an apparent tax protester, was indicted for tax evasion. At trial, he refused to take the oath to tell the truth. The trial court consequently refused to permit him to testify in his defense. He was convicted, and he appealed.

ISSUE: May one testify if one refuses to swear to tell the truth?

HOLDING AND DECISION: (Gee, J.) No. One may not testify if one refuses to swear to tell the truth. Fed. R. Evid. 603 clearly requires that, before testifying, every witness will swear to tell the truth, on oath or affirmation. Therefore, taking the oath is a precondition to the right to testify. Since Fowler (D) refused to take the oath, the district court properly did not permit him to testify. Affirmed.

ANALYSIS

The requirement that a witness take an oath generally has been held to go beyond merely reciting the words. A witness generally must understand the import of the words. For this reason, insanity or infancy will usually disqualify a witness if the condition makes it impossible to understand the meaning of the words.

Quicknotes

OATH The attestation by a witness assuring the court that he or she understands the need for truthfulness and will testify accordingly.

Ricketts v. Delaware

Convicted rapist (D) v. State (P)

Del. Sup. Ct., 488 A.2d 856 (1985)

NATURE OF CASE: Appeal of conviction for rape.

FACT SUMMARY: A young child was permitted to testify against Ricketts (D) after she demonstrated an understanding of the concepts of truth and falsehood.

RULE OF LAW

A young child may testify if the child demonstrates an understanding of the concepts of truth and falsehood.

FACTS: Ricketts (D) was accused of raping an acquaintance's five-year-old daughter. At trial, the child was examined by the court and counsel as to her understanding of the concepts of truth and falsehood. While she didn't understand the concept of perjury, she clearly understood the difference between the truth and a lie. The court permitted her to testify. Ricketts (D) was convicted, and he appealed.

ISSUE: May a young child testify if the child demonstrates an understanding of the concepts of truth and falsehood?

HOLDING AND DECISION: (Moore, J.) Yes. A young child may testify if the child demonstrates an understanding of the concepts of truth and falsehood. Under Delaware evidence rules, anyone is presumed to be competent to testify, provided he or she takes the oath and demonstrates a basic understanding as to its meaning. The mental or moral capacity of the witness goes to credibility, not competency. Here, the child did demonstrate an understanding of the concept of truth, and she was, therefore, competent. Affirmed.

ANALYSIS

At common law, young children were presumed incompetent to testify. Some jurisdictions still retain vestiges of this. The federal rules, however, have completely jettisoned this. The Delaware rules here were patterned after the federal rules.

Quicknotes

COMPETENCY TO TESTIFY Those qualifications necessary for a witness to possess in order to be permitted to give testimony at a trial consistent with the requirements of law.

Tanner v. United States

Convicted felon (D) v. Federal government (P)

483 U.S.107 (1987)

NATURE OF CASE: Review of order denying new trial in criminal prosecution.

FACT SUMMARY: Tanner (D) contended that he was entitled to a new trial because of juror testimony to the effect that several jurors sat while intoxicated.

RULE OF LAW

Juror testimony to the effect that jurors sat while intoxicated is an insufficient basis upon which to grant a new trial.

FACTS: Tanner (D) was tried and convicted of mail fraud. Following the trial, two jurors stepped forward and told Tanner's (D) attorney of the use by several jurors of intoxicating substances, namely, beer, wine, marijuana, and cocaine. Based on affidavits executed by the jurors, Tanner moved for a new trial. The district court denied the motion, and the court of appeals affirmed. Tanner (D) petitioned for certiorari to the United States Supreme Court.

ISSUE: Is juror testimony to the effect that jurors sat while intoxicated a sufficient basis upon which to grant a new trial?

HOLDING AND DECISION: (O'Connor, J.) No. Juror testimony to the effect that jurors sat while intoxicated is an insufficient basis upon which to grant a new trial. By the beginning of the twentieth century, the rule had been clearly established that juror testimony could not be admitted to impeach a verdict. This rule was based on the necessity of ensuring the finality of jury verdicts. To hold otherwise would open up juries to post-verdict probing by the losing party, with the concomitant possibility of verdicts being set aside at any time. It is doubtful if the jury system could survive this. An exception has been recognized: juror testimony regarding improper external influences on a jury may be admitted to impeach a verdict. However, juror intoxication cannot be considered an external influence, as no outside actor is involved. For this reason, the district court properly rejected Tanner's (D) motion for a new trial. Affirmed.

ANALYSIS

The Court did not address the issue of what the result might be if nonjuror witnesses offered evidence of improper juror conduct. Generally, the rules regarding impeachment of jury verdicts by evidence apart from juror testimony are less rigid than that governing juror testimony. Nonetheless, courts are loath to upset verdicts based on juror misconduct.

CHAPTER 7

Direct and Cross-Examination Revisited

Quick Reference Rules of Law

PAGE

1. *Baker v. State.* Anything, including a memorandum made by another or a record that does not otherwise meet the standards for a record of past recollection, can be used to refresh a witness's recollection of an event. 54

Baker v. State

Convicted felon (D) v. Government (P)

Md. Ct. App., 371 A.2d 699 (1977)

NATURE OF CASE: Appeal from a conviction for first-degree murder and robbery.

FACT SUMMARY: Baker's (D) counsel was not permitted to use a police report prepared by another officer to refresh the recollection of Officer Bolton while he was on the stand testifying.

RULE OF LAW

Anything, including a memorandum made by another or a record that does not otherwise meet the standards for a record of past recollection, can be used to refresh a witness's recollection of an event.

FACTS: Baker (D) was convicted of robbery and murder in the first degree. On appeal therefrom, she argued that the trial judge had erred in refusing her counsel the opportunity to refresh the present recollection of a police officer who was testifying by showing him a report written by a fellow officer. In cross-examining Officer Bolton, Baker's (D) counsel sought to elicit from him the fact that the crime victim confronted Baker (D) and stated that she was not one of the persons who had attacked and robbed him. Officer Bolton had stated he did not remember whom it was the crime victim had so confronted, and Baker's (D) counsel sought to have him look at a police report prepared by another officer to refresh his memory on that point. The judge did not allow it.

ISSUE: Can anything, including a memorandum made by another or a record that does not otherwise meet the standards for a record of past recollection, be used to refresh a witness's recollection of an event?

HOLDING AND DECISION: (Moylan, J.) Yes. Anything, including a memorandum made by another or a record that does not otherwise meet the standards for a record of past recollection, can be used to refresh a witness's recollection of an event. This is because the stimulus that is used to revive a witness's dormant memory is not itself admitted in evidence. Thus, the stimulus is not to be confused with documents admitted into evidence as embodiments of past recollections recorded and not subject to the same stringent rules of admission. All that is required is that the stimulus ignite the flash of accurate recall, i.e., that it accomplished the revival that is sought. The stimulus used need not even be in writing. Even if it is a writing, it need not have ever been read by the witness before the witness sees it at trial nor does the witness have to vouch for it or its accuracy. Under these principles, Baker's (D) counsel should have been allowed to refresh Officer Bolton's present recollection with a fellow officer's report. Reversed and remanded for a new trial.

ANALYSIS

Whatever memory aid is used to refresh a witness's recollection, it is always subject to inspection by the opposing party, which has the right to show it to the jury. The party seeking to use the memory aid may not submit it to the jury for its inspection, however, unless it constitutes evidence that is otherwise admissible.

Quicknotes

PAST RECOLLECTION RECORDED An exception to the hearsay rule for statements contained in a document as to which the witness no longer has recollection.

REFRESHMENT OF MEMORY The use of a document to refresh the recollection of a witness at trial as to past events.

CHAPTER 8

Impeachment of Witnesses

Quick Reference Rules of Law

United States v. Abel

Federal government (P) v. Convicted bank robber (D)

469 U.S. 45 (1984)

NATURE OF CASE: Appeal from a bank-robbery conviction.

FACT SUMMARY: The Court of Appeals for the Ninth Circuit overturned Abel's (D) conviction on the basis that evidence produced to impeach a defense witness was improper in that it suggested the witness was committing perjury due to his membership in a particular organization.

RULE OF LAW

Evidence that is sufficiently probative of a witness's possible bias for or against a party warrants its admission into evidence.

FACTS: Abel (D) was arrested and tried for bank robbery. One accomplice who pleaded guilty prior to trial, Ehle, agreed to testify against Abel (D) at his trial. At trial, Ehle implicated Abel (D), and Abel (D) called a Robert Mills, a cellmate of Ehle in prison. Mills testified that Ehle had admitted to him that he intended to implicate Abel (D) falsely in order to receive more favorable treatment from the government. Ehle was then called back to the stand to testify that he, Mills, and Abel (D) were members of a prison gang that required its members to deny the existence of the organization and to commit perjury on each other's behalf. This evidence was presented to impeach Mills's prior testimony. Abel (D) objected to the testimony concerning the prison gang on the basis that it was improper impeachment based upon the witness's participation in an organization. Abel (D) was convicted and appealed. The Court of Appeals for the Ninth Circuit overturned the conviction, and the United States Supreme Court granted review.

ISSUE: Is evidence that is sufficiently probative of a witness's possible bias for or against a party admissible?

HOLDING AND DECISION: (Rehnquist, J.) Yes. Evidence that is sufficiently probative of a witness's possible bias for or against a party warrants its admission into evidence. The fact that Mills belonged to a perjurious organization gives rise to a clear inference that he may be perjuring himself in court. Weighing credibility being the most important aspect of the trier of fact's duty, such evidence was clearly relevant and clearly admissible to show bias. The tremendous impact of bias upon a witness's credibility requires that such evidence be admitted. As a result, the trial court properly admitted the evidence, and the conviction must stand. The decision of the court of appeals is reversed.

ANALYSIS

Courts often give wide range in terms of admitting evidence of bias. Because the weight of a witness's testimony is the most important aspect of the trial, any evidence that reasonably could show an inclination towards slanting the facts for or against a particular party is almost always relevant. The objection to such evidence properly falls within the argument that such evidence is so inflammatory, or so likely to mislead or confuse the jury, that its probative value is outweighed by its prejudicial impact. In this case, the Court found that the probative value of the evidence, although somewhat inflammatory, clearly outweighed its prejudicial impact, and therefore admitted the evidence.

Quicknotes

IMPEACHMENT The discrediting of a witness by offering evidence to show that the witness lacks credibility.

United States v. Manske

Federal government (P) v. Convicted drug dealer (D)

186 F.3d 770 (7th Cir. 1999)

NATURE OF CASE: Appeal from conviction for conspiracy to distribute cocaine.

FACT SUMMARY: Manske (D) contended that the trial judge erred in granting the Government's (P) in limine motion to prevent cross-examination of the Government's (P) key witness as to the fact that the witness, who was himself a drug dealer had, in prior trials on several occasions, told potential witnesses he would kill them if they testified against him.

RULE OF LAW

A threat to cause physical harm to a person who testifies is sufficiently probative of truthfulness to permit cross-examination of the matter under Fed. R. Evid. 608(b).

FACTS: Manske (D) was convicted for conspiracy to distribute cocaine. At trial, the court granted the Government's (P) motion in limine to prevent Manske's attorney from cross-examining the prosecution's key witness concerning the fact that the witness, who was himself a drug dealer, had in prior trials, on several occasions, told potential witnesses he would kill them if they testified against him. In support of its motion, the Government (P) had successfully argued that threatening to cause physical harm to a person who testifies is not sufficiently probative of truthfulness to permit cross-examination of the matter under Fed. R. Evid. 608(b). Manske (D) appealed, contending that threats calculated to encourage people to break the law are probative of truthfulness under Fed. R. Evid. 608(b).

ISSUE: Is a threat to cause physical harm to a person who testifies sufficiently probative of truthfulness to permit cross-examination of the matter under Fed. R. Evid. 608(b)?

HOLDING AND DECISION: (Flaum, J.) Yes. A threat to cause physical harm to a person who testifies is sufficiently probative of truthfulness to permit cross-examination of the matter under Fed. R. Evid. 608(b). Under Fed. R. Evid. 608(b), a witness's specific instances of conduct may only be raised on cross-examination if they are probative of truthfulness or untruthfulness. Here, Pszeniczka, as the Government's (P) prime witness, gave highly damaging testimony against Manske (D). The federal district court, however, did not permit Manske (D) to cross-examine Pszeniczka about the latter's statements to potential witnesses in an earlier trial that he would kill them if they testified against him. A witness testified in an earlier trial that Pszeniczka confronted and threatened her for talking to the police, as did other witnesses. Here, the trial judge was incorrect in accepting the Government's (P) argument that such statements by Pszeniczka tended only to show a propensity for violence but are not conduct probative of truthfulness. On the contrary, threats calculated to encourage people to break the law are probative of truthfulness. These threats supported the defense theory that the Government's (P) case rested on an elaborate set-up depending on testimony by Pszeniczka and others who were afraid to contradict him. As a practical matter, it is hard to distinguish between untruthfulness and dishonesty. Reversed and remanded for a new trial.

ANALYSIS

In rejecting the Government's (P) argument in the *Manske* case that the errors were harmless, the court considered the importance of the testimony, the presence or absence of corroborating or contradictory evidence, the extent of cross-examination, and the strength of the Government's (P) case. Here, the appellate court reversed the conviction since the errors impacted the cross-examination of three of the Government's (P) key witnesses and assessing one of those witnesses' credibility was "critical" because of the lack of physical evidence.

Quicknotes

MOTION IN LIMINE Motion by one party brought prior to trial to exclude the potential introduction of prejudicial evidence.

Luce v. United States

Convicted drug dealer (D) v. Federal government (P)

469 U.S. 38 (1984)

NATURE OF CASE: Appeal from conviction for conspiracy and possession of cocaine with intent to distribute.

FACT SUMMARY: In the Government's (P) action against Luce (D) for conspiracy and possession of cocaine with intent to distribute, Luce contended that the district court's ruling denying Luce's motion to forbid the use of a prior conviction to impeach his credibility was an abuse of discretion.

RULE OF LAW

To raise and preserve for review the claim of improper impeachment with a prior conviction, a defendant must testify at trial.

FACTS: Luce (D) was indicted on charges of conspiracy and possession of cocaine with intent to distribute, in violation of 21 U.S.C. §§46 and 841(a)(1). During his trial, Luce (D) moved for a ruling to preclude the Government (P) from using a 1974 state conviction to impeach him if he testified. Luce (D) made no commitment that he would testify if the motion was granted and did not make a proffer to the court as to what his testimony would be. In opposing the motion, the Government (P) represented that the conviction was for a serious crime: possession of a controlled substance. The district court ruled that the prior conviction fell within the category of permissible impeachment evidence under Fed. R. Evid. 609(a). Luce (D) did not testify, and the jury returned a guilty verdict. The Sixth Circuit Court of Appeals affirmed the district court's decision. The court of appeals refused to consider Luce's (D) contention that the district court abused its discretion in denying Luce's motion in limine without making a specific finding that the probative value of the prior conviction outweighed its prejudicial effect. The court of appeals held that when a defendant does not testify, the court will not review the district court's in limine ruling.

ISSUE: To raise and preserve for review the claim of improper impeachment with a prior conviction, must a defendant testify at trial?

HOLDING AND DECISION: (Burger, C.J.) Yes. To raise and preserve for review the claim of improper impeachment with a prior conviction, a defendant must testify at trial. Under Fed. R. Evid. 609(a)(1), which directs the court to weigh the probative value of a prior conviction against the prejudicial effect to the defendant, to perform such balancing a court must know the precise nature of the defendant's testimony, which is unknowable when, as here, a defendant does not testify. Were in limine rulings under Rule 609(a) reviewable on appeal, almost any error would result in the windfall of automatic reversal. Requiring Luce (D) to testify in order to preserve Fed. R. Evid. 609(a) claims will enable the reviewing court to determine the impact any erroneous impeachment many have had in light of the record as a whole. Affirmed.

ANALYSIS

As a method of impeachment, evidence of conviction of a crime is significant only because it stands as proof of the commission of the underlying criminal act. There is little disagreement from the general proposition that at least some crimes are relevant to credibility. There is, however, much disagreement among cases and commentators about which crimes are usable for this purpose. Traditionally, use of felonies has been accepted for crimes involving dishonesty or false statement without regard to the grade of the offense.

Quicknotes

FED. R. EVID. 609 Outlines the rules for attacking a witness's character for truthfulness by evidence of a criminal conviction.

IMPEACHMENT The discrediting of a witness by offering evidence to show that the witness lacks credibility.

MOTION IN LIMINE Motion by one party brought prior to trial to exclude the potential introduction of prejudicial evidence.

United States v. Webster

Federal government (P) v. Convicted robber (D)

734 F.2d 1191 (7th Cir. 1984)

NATURE OF CASE: Appeal from conviction of aiding and abetting a bank robbery and receiving stolen funds.

FACT SUMMARY: Webster (D) appealed from his conviction of aiding and abetting a bank robbery and receiving stolen funds, arguing it was impermissible to call a hostile witness for the purpose of introducing inadmissible evidence for impeachment purposes.

RULE OF LAW

Impeachment by prior inconsistent statement is impermissible if used to get otherwise inadmissible evidence before the jury.

FACTS: Webster (D) was accused of aiding and abetting a bank robbery and receiving stolen funds. The Government (P) called King as a witness against Webster (D). King had pled guilty to the bank robbery and been sentenced to a long prison term. Upon King's giving testimony that if believed would have exculpated Webster (D), the Government (P) introduced King's prior inconsistent statements to the FBI inculpating Webster (D). The Government (P) attempted to introduce King's testimony outside the jury, but defense counsel objected. Webster (D) was convicted and appealed, contending it was impermissible to call a hostile witness for the purpose of introducing inadmissible evidence for impeachment purposes.

ISSUE: Is impeachment by prior inconsistent statement permissible if used to get otherwise inadmissible evidence before the jury?

HOLDING AND DECISION: (Posner, J.) No. Impeachment by prior inconsistent statement is impermissible if used to get otherwise inadmissible evidence before the jury. Using evidence in this way places hearsay evidence as substantive evidence against Webster (D), a result neither contemplated nor authorized by Fed. R. Evid. 607. Here, however, there was no bad faith on the part of the Government (P). The prosecutor did not know what King would say and offered to examine King outside the presence of the jury. The good faith standard strikes the proper balance among competing interests. Affirmed.

ANALYSIS

Many articles have been written on the delicate subject of impeaching one's own witness. Some argue Webster's (D) position in the present case, that the courts should require surprise and harm before impeachment by prior inconsistent statement is allowed. See 3A J. Wigmore, Evidence §§96-918 (Chadburn rev. 1970) for background on the issue of impeaching one's own witness.

Quicknotes

IMPEACHMENT The discrediting of a witness by offering evidence to show that the witness lacks credibility.

Harris v. New York

Convicted drug dealer (D) v. State (P)

401 U.S. 222 (1971)

NATURE OF CASE: Appeal from conviction for selling narcotics.

FACT SUMMARY: Statements obtained in violation of *Miranda v. Arizona*, 384 U.S. 436 (1966), were admitted in order to impeach Harris's (D) testimony.

RULE OF LAW

Statements obtained in violation of a defendant's *Miranda* rights may be admitted for impeachment purposes.

FACTS: Harris (D) was arrested for selling heroin. He was not given his *Miranda* rights. *Miranda v. Arizona*, 384 U.S. 436 (1966). While in custody, he admitted that he was selling heroin. At trial Harris (D) took the stand on his own behalf and testified that all he had sold was baking powder in an attempt to defraud the purchaser. He stated that the previously submitted evidence showing that the substance had been heroin had been "cooked up" to frame him. On cross-examination, the prosecution asked him if he had made certain statements during interrogation by the police showing that the bag contained heroin. These statements had not been introduced by the prosecution during its case and are admitted to having been obtained in derogation of Harris's (D) *Miranda* rights. The prosecution stated that they were being used solely for impeachment. The questions were allowed, and Harris (D) was convicted. He claimed that these statements were inadmissible for any purpose.

ISSUE: Are statements obtained in violation of a defendant's *Miranda* admissible for impeachment purposes?

HOLDING AND DECISION: (Burger, C.J.) Yes. Statements obtained in violation of a defendant's *Miranda* rights may be admitted for impeachment purposes. A defendant cannot perjure him- or herself with impunity because impeachment evidence was obtained in derogation of a constitutionally protected right. The court properly admitted the evidence and gave adequate limiting instructions on the fact that it was only to be considered for impeachment purposes. The conviction is affirmed.

DISSENT: (Brennan, J.) The Constitution denies the State (P) the use of an accused's inadmissible statements on cross-examination to impeach the credibility of an accused's testimony given in his or her own defense. The Constitution guarantees a defendant the fullest opportunity to meet the accusation against him or her. An accused must be free to deny all the elements of the case against him or her without thereby giving leave to the government to introduce by way of rebuttal evidence illegally secured and, therefore, not available for its case-in-chief. In this regard, there must be no distinction between statements used on direct as opposed to cross-examination.

ANALYSIS

As a general rule, no evidence is admissible that resulted from illegal police procedures. It is excluded under the "fruits of the poisonous tree" doctrine. However, the rationale of *Harris* has been extended to other excluded evidence areas for impeachment purposes. The same rationale has been used to support these decisions, i.e., perjury should not be allowed. See *Walder v. U.S.*, 347 U.S. 62 (1954).

Quicknotes

FRUIT OF THE POISONOUS TREE Doctrine that evidence obtained as a result of illegal procedures is tainted and is usually inadmissible at trial.

IMPEACHMENT The discrediting of a witness by offering evidence to show that the witness lacks credibility.

***MIRANDA* WARNINGS** Specified warnings that must be communicated to a person prior to a custodial interrogation; in the absence of the communication of such warnings, any communications made during the interrogation are inadmissible at trial.

United States v. Havens

Federal government (P) v. Convicted drug dealer (D)

446 U.S. 620 (1980)

NATURE OF CASE: Appeal of drug-related conviction.

FACT SUMMARY: The Government (P) used suppressed evidence to impeach testimony given by Havens (D) on cross-examination.

RULE OF LAW

Suppressed evidence may be used to impeach testimony given by a criminal defendant on cross-examination.

FACTS: Havens (D) was arrested when companion McLeroth was found by U.S. Customs to have cocaine hidden in pockets sewn onto an undershirt he wore. A T-shirt with cutout patterns matching the pockets sewn onto McLeroth's shirt was found in Havens's (D) suitcase. At trial, the court suppressed the T-shirt. Havens (D), testifying in his defense, denied knowledge of the T-shirt during cross-examination. In rebuttal, the Government (P) introduced the shirt over Havens's (D) objection. Havens (D) was convicted, but the court of appeals reversed, holding that suppressed evidence could be admitted only in rebuttal to contradict testimony given on direct. The United States Supreme Court granted certiorari.

ISSUE: May suppressed evidence be used to impeach testimony given by a criminal defendant on cross-examination?

HOLDING AND DECISION: (White, J.) Yes. Suppressed evidence may be used to impeach testimony given by a criminal defendant on cross-examination. This Court has already held that such evidence may be introduced to rebut testimony given on direct. The Court ruled that the purpose of the exclusionary rule is fully served by denying the Government (P) the use of illegally obtained evidence in its case-in-chief. If a defendant chooses to testify and lies, the Government (P) should be able to rebut the testimony with any available means; the truth-finding function of the trial process demands it. There is no reason not to apply this to cross-examination testimony, as a defendant is under the same obligation to tell the truth on cross. The evidence here was, therefore, properly admitted. Reversed and remanded.

DISSENT: (Brennan, J.) A prosecutor should not be allowed to use cross-examination as a vehicle to gain admission to otherwise inadmissible evidence.

ANALYSIS

The Court has never come close to doing away with the exclusionary rule, but since the late 1960s has availed itself of numerous opportunities to limit it. The present case is an illustration of this. Another such case was *Harris v. New York*, 401 U.S. 222 (1971), which permits inadmissible statements to be used for impeachment.

Quicknotes

IMPEACHMENT The discrediting of a witness by offering evidence to show that the witness lacks credibility.

CHAPTER 9

Opinion and Expert Testimony; Scientific Evidence

Quick Reference Rules of Law

Daubert v. Merrell Dow Pharmaceuticals

Drug-related injured person (P) v. Pharmaceutical company (D)

509 U.S. 579 (1993)

NATURE OF CASE: Appeal from a grant of defendant's motion for summary judgment in an action to recover damages for personal injuries.

FACT SUMMARY: In Daubert's (P) suit to recover damages for serious birth defects allegedly caused by a drug marketed by Merrell Dow Pharmaceuticals (Merrell Dow) (D), the court granted Merrell Dow's (D) motion for summary judgment after applying the general acceptance, or *Frye*, rule to the scientific evidence of Daubert's (P) expert witnesses.

RULE OF LAW

If scientific knowledge will assist the trier of fact to understand the evidence or to determine a fact in issue, a witness qualified as an expert by knowledge, skill, experience, training, or education may testify thereto in the form of an opinion or otherwise.

FACTS: Jason Daubert (P) and Eric Schuller (P) brought this suit for damages, alleging that their serious birth defects had been caused by their mothers' ingestion of Bendectin, a drug marketed by Merrell Dow Pharmaceuticals (Merrell Dow) (D). Merrell Dow (D) moved for summary judgment, submitting an affidavit by its expert witness, who concluded, after reviewing more than 30 published studies, that maternal use of Bendectin during the first trimester of pregnancy was not a risk factor for human birth defects. Daubert's (P) and Schuller's (P) eight experts conducted their own studies and reanalyzed previously published studies, concluding that Bendectin can cause birth defects. The court granted Merrell Dow's (D) motion for summary judgment, holding that scientific evidence must be generally accepted to be admissible. The Ninth Circuit Court of Appeals affirmed. Daubert (P) and Schuller (P) appealed.

ISSUE: If scientific knowledge will assist the trier of fact to understand the evidence or to determine a fact in issue, may a witness qualified as an expert by knowledge, skill, experience, training, or education testify thereto in the form of an opinion or otherwise?

HOLDING AND DECISION: (Blackmun, J.) Yes. If scientific knowledge will assist the trier of fact to understand the evidence or to determine a fact in issue, a witness qualified as an expert by knowledge, skill, experience, training, or education may testify thereto in the form of an opinion or otherwise. The general acceptance test established by *Frye v. United States*, 293 F. 1013 (D.C. Cir. 1923), has been displaced by the Federal Rules of Evidence. The current inquiry to be made under Fed. R. Evid. 702 is the scientific validity, and thus the evidentiary relevance and reliability, of the principles underlying a proposed submission. Unlike an ordinary witness, an expert is permitted wide latitude to offer opinions. Accordingly, the judgment of the court of appeals is vacated, and the case is remanded for further proceedings.

CONCURRENCE AND DISSENT: (Rehnquist, C.J.) The Court correctly concluded that the enactment of the Federal Rules Evidence replaced the "general acceptance" doctrine of *Frye v. United States*, 293 F. 1013 (D.C. Cir. 1923). The Court went too far, however, in concocting a new test based only on general principles and observations, and not upon the facts of the case at hand. The standards the majority set out as a substitute for the Frye "general acceptance" test is not that different from it, except they are even vaguer. While judges do need to make some determinations as to the relevance and validity of scientific expert testimony, it is beyond their experience and resources to expect them to go through the analysis the majority describes. It is certain that lower federal courts will have a very difficult time interpreting not only the scientific evidence they are faced with, but also the majority opinion.

ANALYSIS

The Federal Rules of Evidence assign to the trial judge the task of ensuring that an expert's testimony both rests on a reliable foundation and is relevant to the task at hand. Pertinent evidence based on scientifically valid principles will satisfy those demands. While publication, peer review, and general acceptance can have a bearing on the court's inquiry, they are not dispositive.

Quicknotes

EXPERT TESTIMONY Testimonial evidence about a complex area of subject matter relevant to trial, presented by a person competent to inform the trier of fact due to specialized knowledge or training.

OPINION EVIDENCE Evidence pertaining to the beliefs of the witness rather than to witness's knowledge of the facts.

Kumho Tire Company, Ltd. v. Carmichael

Tire manufacturer and distributor (D) v. Accident victim (P)

526 U.S. 137 (1998)

NATURE OF CASE: Review of order declaring evidence inadmissible and judgment for defendant.

FACT SUMMARY: Carmichael (P) claimed that his expert-witness testimony was improperly excluded at trial and successfully appealed the trial court's application of the *Daubert* factors to determine the admissibility of technical evidence.

RULE OF LAW

A trial court must examine the reliability of expert testimony for not only "scientific" knowledge but "technical" or "other specialized" knowledge as well and may flexibly apply one or more of *Daubert's* specific factors to determine the admissibility of a technical expert's testimony based on its relevancy and reliability.

FACTS: The right rear tire on Carmichael's (P) minivan blew out and caused an accident in which one passenger died and others were severely injured. Carmichael (P) alleged that the tire was defective and sued the manufacturer, Kumho Tire Company, Ltd. (Kumho) (D). Carmichael (P) rested his case in significant part upon deposition testimony provided by an expert in tire-failure analysis, who intended to testify in support of his conclusion. Kumho's (D) motion to exclude that testimony was granted on the ground the tire expert's methodology failed Fed. R. Evid. 702's reliability requirement. The specific factors discussed in *Daubert v. Merrell Dow Pharmaceuticals, Inc.*, 509 U.S. 579 (1993), to determine whether scientific expert testimony is both relevant and reliable were applied by the court. These factors include testing, peer review, error rules, and the "acceptability" in the relevant scientific community. The court agreed with Kumho (D) that it should act as a *Daubert*-type gatekeeper, even though one might consider the testimony technical, rather than scientific. Carmichael's (P) motion for reconsideration was then granted, but the court later affirmed its earlier order and granted Kumho's (D) motion for summary judgment. The Eleventh Circuit Court of Appeals reversed, concluding that the testimony fell outside the scope of *Daubert*, whose holding was expressly limited to the application of scientific principles, and not to skill or experience-based observation. Kumho (D) appealed, and the United States Supreme Court granted certiorari.

ISSUE: Must a trial court examine the reliability of expert testimony for not only "scientific" knowledge, but "technical" or "other specialized" knowledge as well and could the court flexibly apply one or more of *Daubert's* specific factors to determine the admissibility of a technical expert's testimony based on its relevancy and reliability?

HOLDING AND DECISION: (Breyer, J.) Yes. A trial court must examine the reliability of expert testimony for not only "scientific" knowledge but "technical" or "other specialized" knowledge as well and may flexibly apply one or more of the specific factors of *Daubert's* specific factors to determine the admissibility of a technical expert's testimony based on its relevancy and reliability. A trial judge has a special obligation to ensure that any and all scientific testimony is not only relevant, but reliable. *Daubert v. Merrell Dow Pharmaceuticals, Inc.*, 509 U.S. 579 (1993), applies to technical or other specialized, non-specific knowledge where expert testimony is being proffered. Thus, some of *Daubert's* questions can help to evaluate the reliability even of experience-based testimony. Whether *Daubert's* specific factors are, or are not, reasonable measures of reliability in a particular case is a matter that the law grants the trial judge broad latitude to determine. The trial judge in this case determined that the testimony fell outside the area where experts might reasonably differ, and where the jury must decide among the conflicting views of different experts, even though the evidence is shaky. The doubts that triggered the trial court's initial inquiry here were reasonable, as was the court's ultimate conclusion. Federal Rule of Evidence 702 grants the district judge the discretionary authority, reviewable for its abuse, to determine reliability in light of the particular facts and circumstances of the particular case. The district court did not abuse its discretionary authority in this case. Reversed.

CONCURRENCE: (Scalia, J.) Trial judges have discretion to "choose among reasonable means" of appraising science. They do not have discretion to perform the gatekeeping responsibility "inadequately."

CONCURRENCE AND DISSENT: (Stevens, J.) The question whether Carlson should have been allowed to testify should be decided by the trial court under the correct standard as set forth in this opinion.

ANALYSIS

Justice Stevens concurred with the first two parts of the court's decision here but dissented from the disposition

Continued on next page.

of the case. He wrote that the question of the exclusion of the expert testimony should be decided by the court of appeals since it involved a study of the record. *Daubert v. Merrell Dow Pharmaceuticals, Inc.*, 509 U.S. 579 (1993), itself made clear that its list of factors was meant to be helpful, not definitive.

Quicknotes

EXPERT TESTIMONY Testimonial evidence about a complex area of subject matter relevant to trial, presented by a person competent to inform the trier of fact due to specialized knowledge or training.

EXPERT WITNESS A witness providing testimony at trial who is specially qualified regarding the particular subject matter involved.

State v. Moore

Government (P) v. Indicted murderer (D)

Mont. Sup. Ct., 885 P.2d 457 (1994)

NATURE OF CASE: Appeal by defendant on ruling on admissibility of deoxyribonucleic acid (DNA) evidence.

FACT SUMMARY: Moore (D) was charged with the murder of Brisbin whose body was never found, although deoxyribonucleic acid (DNA) analysis of blood and muscle tissue found in Moore's car were linked to the victim.

RULE OF LAW

Deoxyribonucleic acid (DNA) evidence obtained using restriction fragment length polymorphism (RFLP) analysis satisfies the standards set out by the United States Supreme Court in *Daubert v. Merrell Dow Pharmaceuticals*, 509 U.S. 579 (1993).

FACTS: Brad Brisbin disappeared without a trace on the morning of November 9, 1990. His body was never recovered, but his wife testified that he was on his way to meet Moore (D) at a truck stop. There was proof that Moore's (D) truck was seen near the location later that same morning. When questioned about Brisbin, Moore (D) gave several conflicting responses as to when and where he had last seen the victim. Small pieces of human brain and muscle tissue were discovered in the cab of Moore's (D) truck. Deoxyribonucleic acid (DNA) studies were conducted on them at two different laboratories using restriction fragment length polymorphism (RFLP) analysis. The findings linked the samples tested to the biological father of the victim's children and to the victim's mother. At trial, the defense filed a motion to exclude this evidence, which was overruled. The defense filed a second motion to exclude testimony describing statistical analysis and correlations that the DNA evidence presented could be linked to the defendant's children. This motion was granted.

ISSUE: Does deoxyribonucleic acid (DNA) evidence obtained using restriction fragment length polymorphism (RFLP) analysis satisfy the standards set out by the United States Supreme Court in *Daubert v. Merrell Dow Pharmaceuticals*, 509 U.S. 579 (1993)?

HOLDING AND DECISION: [No judge listed in casebook excerpt.] Yes. Deoxyribonucleic acid (DNA) evidence obtained using restriction fragment length polymorphism (RFLP) analysis satisfies the standards set out by the United States Supreme Court in *Daubert v. Merrell Dow Pharmaceuticals*, 509 U.S. 579 (1993). Although there may be slight inconsistencies in test results, these do not require exclusion of the evidence. DNA evidence is of great value for forensic purposes because no two individuals have the identical DNA, with the exception of identical twins. In addition, because the defense previously filed a motion to exclude statistical analysis on the probability of a match of the DNA evidence, they are prevented from claiming at this time that keeping out this data would be misleading. Affirmed.

ANALYSIS

The holding in *Moore* is significant because it sets a precedent for the acceptance of certain types of deoxyribonucleic acid (DNA) evidence. It has been cited in numerous states and given consideration. It remains an important reference as DNA technologies progress and new types of genetic mapping are developed.

CHAPTER 10

Burdens of Proof and Presumptions

Quick Reference Rules of Law

Sandstrom v. Montana

Murderer (D) v. State (P)

442 U.S. 510 (1979)

NATURE OF CASE: Appeal from a conviction of "deliberate homicide."

FACT SUMMARY: At Sandstrom's (D) trial for deliberate homicide, for which "intent" is an element, the jury was instructed that the law presumed a person intends the ordinary consequences of his acts.

RULE OF LAW

In a case in which intent is an element of the crime charged, due process prohibits instructing the jury that "the law presumes a person intended the ordinary consequences of his voluntary acts."

FACTS: After a jury instruction that "the law presumes that a person intends the ordinary consequences of his voluntary acts," Sandstrom (D) was convicted of "deliberate homicide" for "purposely or knowingly causing the death of Annie Jessen." Sandstrom's (D) defense had been that a personality disorder aggravated by alcohol consumption prevented his acting "purposely" or "knowingly." The Montana Supreme Court, hearing Sandstrom's (D) appeal, agreed with his contention that *Mullaney v. Wilbur*, 421 U.S. 684 (1975), *In re Winship*, 397 U.S. 358 (1970), and *Patterson v. New York*, 432 U.S. 197 (1977), held that due process prohibited a state from shifting to a defendant the burden of disproving an element of the crime charged. However, it viewed the instruction at issue as having merely placed on Sandstrom (D) the burden of producing some evidence that he did not intend the ordinary consequences of his acts and not as having required him to disprove that he acted "purposely" or "knowingly." Thus, it upheld the conviction.

ISSUE: In a case in which intent is an element of the crime charged, does due process prohibit instructing the jury that "the law presumes a person intended the ordinary consequences of his acts?"

HOLDING AND DECISION: (Brennan, J.) Yes. In a case in which intent is an element of the crime charged, due process prohibits instructing the jury that "the law presumes a person intended the ordinary consequences of his voluntary acts." Due process requires that a state prove every element of a criminal offense beyond a reasonable doubt, and this prohibits instructing the jury, in a case in which intent is an element of the crime charged, that "the law presumes that a person intended the ordinary consequences of his voluntary acts." In this case, a reasonable juror could have given the presumption at issue conclusive or persuasion-shifting effect, and that would violate the Due Process Clause by alleviating the state's burden of proving one element of the crime charged. Reversed and remanded.

ANALYSIS

In Burr W. Jones's *The Law of Evidence*, vol. 1, §§9-10, pp. 16-20 (5th ed. 1958), the author sees the use of the word "presumption" as indicating that a particular conclusion must be drawn on the basis of particular proved facts unless and until it is rebutted by some evidence. Use of the word "inference," however, permits the jury to choose whether or not to draw the conclusion.

Quicknotes

DUE PROCESS CLAUSE Language in the Fifth and Fourteenth Amendments to the U.S. Constitution, providing that no person shall be deprived of "life, liberty, or property, without due process of law."

PRESUMPTION A rule of law requiring the court to presume certain facts to be true based on the existence of other facts, thereby shifting the burden of proof to the party against whom the presumption is asserted to rebut.

County of Ulster v. Allen

Government (P) v. Convict (D)

442 U.S. 140 (1979)

NATURE OF CASE: Appeal from affirmance of issuance of habeas corpus.

FACT SUMMARY: Allen (D) claimed his criminal conviction was obtained by use of an unconstitutional statutory presumption making the presence of a firearm in an automobile presumptive evidence of its illegal possession by all persons then occupying the vehicle.

RULE OF LAW

For a permissible presumption to be constitutional, there must be a rational connection between the basic facts the prosecution proved and the ultimate fact presumed, and the ultimate fact presumed must more likely than not flow from the facts proved.

FACTS: New York law made the presence of a firearm in an automobile presumptive evidence of its illegal possession by all persons then occupying the vehicle. Allen (D) and others suffered a criminal conviction in a trial in which this statutory presumption was applied under instructions that were vague but that arguably suggested it was permissible rather than mandatory. After a writ of habeas corpus was granted on the ground the statute was unconstitutional and an appellate affirmance of that decision, the United States Supreme Court addressed the question.

ISSUE: Does the constitutionality of a permissible presumption depend on there being a rational connection between the basic facts the prosecution proved and the ultimate fact presumed, and on the ultimate fact presumed being more likely than not to flow from the facts proved?

HOLDING AND DECISION: (Stevens, J.) Yes. For a permissible presumption to be constitutional there must be a rational connection between the basic facts the prosecution proved and the ultimate fact presumed, and the ultimate fact presumed must more likely than not flow from the facts proved. The circumstances of this case indicate the presumption at issue was treated as being permissive, so the argument that a reasonable-doubt standard should be used to assess its constitutional validity simply will not stand. Under the appropriate standard for permissive presumptions, the presumption here was constitutional. Reversed.

DISSENT: (Powell, J.) This presumption violates due process because it does not fairly reflect what common sense and experience tell us about passengers in automobiles and the possession of handguns.

ANALYSIS

The United States Supreme Court has held that the existence of other evidence in the record sufficient to support a conviction is relevant in analyzing a purely permissive presumption but not in analyzing a mandatory presumption. *Turner v. United States*, 319 U.S. 463 (1970); *Leary v. United States*, 395 U.S. 6 (1969); *United States v. Romano*, 382 U.S. 136 (1965).

Quicknotes

PRESUMPTION A rule of law requiring the court to presume certain facts to be true based on the existence of other facts, thereby shifting the burden of proof to the party against whom the presumption is asserted to rebut.

CHAPTER 11

Judicial Notice

Quick Reference Rules of Law

Government of the Virgin Islands v. Gereau

Government (P) v. Convicted felon (D)

523 F.2d 140 (3d Cir. 1975)

NATURE OF CASE: Appeal of multiple felony conviction.

FACT SUMMARY: A court took judicial notice of a fact personally known to the sitting judge.

RULE OF LAW

A court may not take judicial notice of a fact merely because the judge has knowledge of that fact in his or her personal capacity.

FACTS: Gereau (D), after a nine-day jury deliberation, was convicted of murder, assault, and robbery. Gereau (D) sought a new trial based on the statements of one juror who testified that another had merely joined in the verdict to be able to go home. That juror denied the statements. The court taking judicial notice of the fact, known to the trial judge that the juror in question liked jury duty, denied the motion. Gereau (D) appealed.

ISSUE: May a court take judicial notice of a fact merely because the judge has knowledge of that fact in his or her personal capacity?

HOLDING AND DECISION: [Judge not stated in casebook excerpt.] No. A court may not take judicial notice of a fact merely because the judge has knowledge of that fact in his or her personal capacity. Facts of which judicial notice may be taken are those beyond a reasonable controversy, either as matters of common knowledge or capable of immediate determination by recourse to indisputably accurate sources. When a fact does not fall within this definition, judicial notice of it may not be taken, even if the judge personally knows it to be true. Here, the motives of the juror were not of the type of fact amenable to judicial notice, and the court's actions were improper. Affirmed.

ANALYSIS

While the Federal Rules of Evidence tend to be broad in terms of admissible evidence, judicial notice is an exception. Fed. R. Evid. 201(b), which covers judicial notice of adjudicative facts, creates an exacting standard. Any fact not plainly self-evident will have a hard time being admitted under the rule.

Quicknotes

JUDICIAL NOTICE The discretion of a court to recognize certain well-known facts as being true, without the necessity of a party introducing evidence to establish the truth of the fact.

United States v. Jones

Federal government (P) v. Wire tapper (D)

580 F.2d 219 (6th Cir. 1978)

NATURE OF CASE: Appeal from acquittal of illegal interception of telephone calls.

FACT SUMMARY: Jones (D) was acquitted of intercepting telephone calls illegally because the Government (P) failed to allege that the maker of the telephone, South Central Bell, was a common carrier providing facilities for interstate communication.

RULE OF LAW

Failure to plead a fact in a criminal proceeding may not be cured by judicial notice.

FACTS: Jones (D) was charged with illegally intercepting telephone conversations by tapping the telephone of his estranged wife. The telephone was made by South Central Bell, part of an international corporation providing communications services throughout the world. The statute under which Jones (D) was charged required that the interception be from equipment of a common carrier providing facilities for the transmission of interstate communications. The Government (P) failed to allege South Central Bell's status as such a carrier and Jones (D) was accordingly acquitted despite a guilty verdict. The Government (P) appealed, seeking to cure the pleading defect by requesting judicial notice of South Central Bell's status.

ISSUE: May failure to plead a fact in a criminal proceeding be cured by judicial notice?

HOLDING AND DECISION: [Judge not stated in casebook excerpt.] No. Failure to plead a fact in a criminal proceeding may not be cured by judicial notice. While the Fed. R. Evid. 201(f) permits the request of judicial notice at any state of a proceeding, even on appeal, the value of judicial notice is different in a criminal proceeding such as this one than in a civil action. In a civil action, the jury must regard judicially noticed facts as conclusively established. However, in a criminal proceeding, the jury must pass on facts that are judicially noticed, despite the notice. Thus, even if judicial notice is taken, in this case of South Central Bell's status as an interstate carrier, the jury would not be required to accept the fact. Thus, failure to plead a fact in a criminal proceeding may not be cured by judicial notice. The jury's right to reject the judicially noticed fact cannot be taken away by granting notice after the jury is discharged. Affirmed.

ANALYSIS

The neglect of the Government's (P) attorney is on the one hand exactly the kind of mistake that Fed. R. Evid. 201(f) is intended to cure by allowing judicial notice on appeal. However, the right of the defendant to have the jury render its verdict with the ability to reject the judicially noticed fact outweighs the policy for correction on appeal. The peculiar result in this case has been criticized.

Quicknotes

JUDICIAL NOTICE The discretion of a court to recognize certain well-known facts as being true, without the necessity of a party introducing evidence to establish the truth of the fact.

Houser v. State

Challenger of statute (P) v. State (D)

Wash. Sup. Ct., 540 P.2d 412 (1975)

NATURE OF CASE: Review of dismissal of action challenging state liquor regulations.

FACT SUMMARY: In considering the rationality of a statute, a court took judicial notice of scientific studies.

RULE OF LAW

Courts may take judicial notice of scientific studies when analyzing a statute.

FACTS: Houser (P) challenged Washington's minimum-age law on alcohol consumption, alleging equal protection violations. In concluding that the law was rationally related to a legitimate governmental purpose, the trial court took judicial notice of certain scientific studies. The trial court granted summary judgment in favor of the State (D). The appellate court affirmed. The Washington Supreme Court granted review.

ISSUE: May courts take judicial notice of scientific studies when analyzing a statute?

HOLDING AND DECISION: (Utter, J.) Yes. Courts may take judicial notice of scientific studies when analyzing a statute. While a court should not judicially notice a controverted scientific treatise or study when resolving a factual dispute, a court may ascertain as it sees fit any fact that is merely a ground for laying down a rule of law. Here, the court had only to conclude that the statute in question was rational. Evidence of its rationality was the fact that scientific studies existed validating the legislative decision. The trial court correctly noticed their existence. It did not, and did not need to, validate their accuracy. Affirmed.

ANALYSIS

In this case, the existence of the studies at issue was relevant. The contents and accuracy of the studies were not. When the existence of something is not at issue, judicial notice may usually be taken of it.

Quicknotes

JUDICIAL NOTICE The discretion of a court to recognize certain well-known facts as being true, without the necessity of a party introducing evidence to establish the truth of the fact.

RATIONAL-BASIS REVIEW A test employed by the court to determine the validity of a statute in equal protection actions, whereby the court determines whether the challenged statute is rationally related to the achievement of a legitimate state interest.

United States v. Gould

Federal government (P) v. Convicted drug offender (D)

536 F.2d 216 (8th Cir. 1976)

NATURE OF CASE: Appeal from conviction for a drug offense.

FACT SUMMARY: Gould (D) challenged the trial court's action in taking judicial notice of the fact that cocaine hydrochloride was a Schedule II controlled substance and instructing the jury hearing his drug case that it had to accept this fact as conclusive.

RULE OF LAW

Under the Federal Rules of Evidence, a court is not precluded from instructing the jury that it must accept as conclusive a "legislative" fact of which the court has taken judicial notice, i.e., a fact, truth, or pronouncement that does not change from case to case but applies universally.

FACTS: On appeal from a cocaine-related drug conviction, Gould (D) argued that the trial court had acted improperly in taking judicial notice of the fact that cocaine hydrochloride was a Schedule II controlled substance and in instructing the jury that it had to accept this fact as conclusive. At trial, there was no direct evidence to indicate that it was a derivative of coca leaves (and thus a Schedule II substance).

ISSUE: Is a federal court precluded by the Federal Rules of Evidence from instructing the jury that it must accept as conclusive a "legislative" fact of which it has taken judicial notice?

HOLDING AND DECISION: [Judge not stated in casebook excerpt.] No. There is nothing in the Federal Rules of Evidence to preclude a court from instructing the jury that it must accept as conclusive a "legislative" fact of which it has properly taken judicial notice. "Legislative" facts are those that involve universal facts, truths, or pronouncements that do not change from case to case, while "adjudicative" facts are those developed in a particular case. The fact that cocaine hydrochloride is derived from coca leaves is, if not common knowledge, at least a matter that is capable of certain, easily accessible and indisputably accurate verification. It is thus a proper subject of judicial notice. Furthermore, it falls within the category of "legislative" facts as opposed to "adjudicative" facts (which are the facts that relate to the parties, their activities, their properties, their businesses—and that normally go to the jury in a jury case). As such, it is not subject to Fed. R. Evid. 201(g), which covers only adjudicative facts in calling for a jury instruction in civil cases that a judicially noticed fact is conclusive but providing that in criminal cases the jury shall be instructed that it may, but is not required to accept as conclusive, a judicially noticed fact. Thus, nothing prevents a court from instructing a jury that it must accept as conclusive the universal fact that cocaine hydrochloride is a derivative of coca. Affirmed.

ANALYSIS

Not all states agree with the attempted distinction between legislative and adjudicative facts. For example, Montana adopted a rule identical to Fed. R. Evid. 201, except that instead of covering only "adjudicative facts" in terms of judicial notice, it covers "all facts" subject to judicial notice. It reasoned that the attempted distinction was confusing and could not be readily made in many situations.

Quicknotes

JUDICIAL NOTICE The discretion of a court to recognize certain well-known facts as being true, without the necessity of a party introducing evidence to establish the truth of the fact.

CHAPTER 12

Privileges

Quick Reference Rules of Law

People v. Meredith

Government (P) v. Convicted felons (D)

Cal. Sup. Ct., 631 P.2d 46 (1981)

NATURE OF CASE: Appeal from conviction for murder and robbery.

FACT SUMMARY: Frank Earl Scott (D), whose communications with his attorney led a defense investigator to find the murder victim's wallet (which was removed but later turned in to the police), maintained that his privilege against self-incrimination barred the investigator from testifying to the location of the wallet.

RULE OF LAW

When defense counsel removes or alters evidence after its location was revealed by defense counsel's client in an attorney-client privileged communication, attorney-client privilege does not prohibit defense counsel from revealing the original location and condition of that evidence.

FACTS: Frank Earl Scott (D) and Michael Meredith (D) were both convicted of the first-degree murder and first-degree robbery of David Wade. When James Schenk, Scott's (D) first appointed attorney visited him in jail, Scott (D) told him that the victim's wallet (which Scott had tried to burn) was in a plastic bag in a burn barrel behind his house. Schenk proceeded to retain an investigator, Stephen Frick, and sent Frick to find the wallet. Frick found the wallet and brought it back to Schenk, who turned it over to police after examining its contents and determining that it contained credit cards in Wade's name. Schenk told the police only that to the best of his knowledge the wallet had belonged to Wade. On appeal, Scott (D) conceded that the wallet itself was admissible but insisted that his privilege against self-incrimination was a bar to Frick's testimony as to where the wallet had been located.

ISSUE: When defense counsel removes or alters evidence after its location was revealed by defense counsel's client in an attorney-client privileged communication, does attorney-client privilege prohibit defense counsel from revealing the original location and condition of the evidence?

HOLDING AND DECISION: (Tobriner, J.) No. When defense counsel removes or alters evidence after its location was revealed by defense counsel's client in an attorney-client privileged communication, attorney-client privilege does not prohibit defense counsel from revealing the original location and condition of that evidence. Normally, the attorney-client privilege is not strictly limited to communications but extends to protect all observations made as a consequence of protected communication. If, therefore, a privileged communication leads defense counsel to some physical evidence, defense counsel's observations thereof are insulated from revelation so long as defense counsel leaves the evidence where he or she discovers it. If, however, defense counsel makes the tactical decision of removing the evidence to examine or test it, the original location and condition of that evidence loses the protection of the privilege. Thus, the location of the wallet was not protected information in this case. Affirmed.

ANALYSIS

As a tactical maneuver designed to prevent the jury from connecting the defendant with the party who "discovered" the evidence (as the result of privileged communications), the defense will sometimes offer to enter into a stipulation, simply informing the jury as to the location or condition of the evidence. The prosecutor cannot refuse simply in the hopes of providing the opportunity for the jury to make such a connection.

Quicknotes

ATTORNEY-CLIENT PRIVILEGE A doctrine precluding the admission into evidence of confidential communications between an attorney and the client made in the course of obtaining professional assistance.

Suburban Sew 'N Sweep v. Swiss-Bernina

Retailer (P) v. Distributor (D)

91 F.R.D. 254 (N.D. Ill. 1981)

NATURE OF CASE: Action for conspiracy and price-fixing.

FACT SUMMARY: Swiss-Bernina (P) contended the attorney-client privilege protected from disclosure documents intended as confidential communications yet thrown in the garbage and retrieved by Suburban Sew 'N Sweep (P).

RULE OF LAW

The attorney-client privilege is waived when adequate safeguards are not employed to protect disclosure.

FACTS: Suburban Sew 'N Sweep (Suburban) (P), a retailer of sewing products distributed by Swiss-Bernina (Swiss) (D), suspected that Swiss (D) was engaging in illegal price-fixing. Because of this, it had its employees search Swiss's (D) garbage for evidence. Over the course of two years, it retrieved several handwritten drafts of letters sent by Swiss's (D) president to its corporate counsel. In pretrial discovery, Swiss (D) attempted to exclude such documents as falling within the attorney-client privilege. The magistrate ordered the documents excluded, and Suburban (P) sought review. It contended any such privilege was waived due to lack of intended confidentiality.

ISSUE: Is the attorney-client privilege waived when adequate safeguards to disclosure are not employed?

HOLDING AND DECISION: (Leighton, J.) Yes. The attorney-client privilege is waived where adequate safeguards against disclosure are not employed. Placing the documents in the garbage indicated a lack of concern about disclosure, which precludes application of the privilege. If the documents were intended to be held confidential, they should have been obliterated or destroyed. Thus, the failure to do so waived the privilege. Reversed.

ANALYSIS

The court rejected any argument that the documents had been obtained as the result of a Fourth Amendment violation. First, no illegal search occurs when the evidence is in the garbage because there is no reasonable expectation of privacy. Second, only government action falls under the Fourth Amendment prohibition.

Quicknotes

ATTORNEY-CLIENT PRIVILEGE A doctrine precluding the admission into evidence of confidential communications between an attorney and the client made in the course of obtaining professional assistance.

FOURTH AMENDMENT Provides that persons be secure as to their person and private belongings against unreasonable searches and seizures.

Upjohn Co. v. United States

Corporation (D) v. Federal government (P)

449 U.S. 383 (1981)

NATURE OF CASE: Appeal from denial of privilege in tax investigation.

FACT SUMMARY: Upjohn Co. (D) claimed the Internal Revenue Service was not entitled to production of its questionnaires to and interviews of Upjohn (D) employees concerning possibly illegal payments made by Upjohn (D), as they were privileged communications and an attorney's work product.

RULE OF LAW

A corporation is entitled to invoke attorney-client privilege over communications between attorneys and both management- and non-management-level employees.

FACTS: In January 1976, independent accountants discovered that a foreign subsidiary of Upjohn Co. (D) had made payments to or for the benefit of foreign government officials. Upjohn's (D) general counsel conducted investigation of these "possibly illegal" payments, which included interviews of all foreign general and area managers, and various other Upjohn (D) employees, and questionnaires to the foreign managers. The Internal Revenue Service conducted its own investigation to determine the tax consequences of the payments. It demanded production of all Upjohn's (D) relevant files, including the questionnaires and memoranda of the interviews. Upjohn (D) claimed these were privileged and protected as the work product of an attorney in anticipation of litigation. Upjohn (D) appealed the enforcement of the summons. The Sixth Circuit Court of Appeals affirmed to the extent that officers and employees not responsible for directing Upjohn's (D) actions in response to legal advice were not "clients" whose communications could come within the attorney-client privilege. The case was remanded to district court for a determination as to who was not within the "control group." The district court was not to consider the work-product doctrine, which the Sixth Circuit found inapplicable to administrative summonses. Upjohn (D) appealed.

ISSUE: Is a corporation entitled to invoke attorney-client privilege over communications between attorneys and both management- and non-management-level employees?

HOLDING AND DECISION: (Rehnquist, J.) Yes. A corporation is entitled to invoke attorney-client privilege over communications between attorneys and both management- and non-management-level employees. The court rejected the "control-group" test adopted by the Sixth Circuit, which grants the attorney-client privilege to only those communications made by employees responsible for directing the corporation's actions in response to legal advice, arguing that it frustrates the very purpose of the privilege by discouraging communication of relevant information by employees of the client corporation to attorneys seeking to render their best legal advice to the corporate control group. Further, the very terms of the test adopted by the court below suggest the unpredictability of its application, as those whose communications receive the privilege must play a "substantial role" in directing corporate actions in response to the advice. Thus, in the case of a corporation claiming the privilege, the control-group test does not govern; whether any particular communication is privileged must be determined on a case-by-case basis. Here, the communications in question were made by Upjohn (D) employees to its (D) counsel at the direction of its (D) officers so that they might get advice from the counsel. Thus, these communications— the questionnaires and notes reflecting responses to interviews— are privileged. Regarding the notes that go beyond recording responses to interviews, Fed. R. Evid. 26 offers special protection to work product that reveals an attorney's mental processes. While a sufficient showing of necessity can overcome protection as to tangible items and documents, a far stronger showing is required as to material revealing a lawyer's mental impressions. Here, the lesser standard was erroneously applied by the district court to the attorney's memoranda of interviews, which went beyond the recording of responses. Reversed and remanded.

ANALYSIS

Before the *Upjohn* case, the weight of authority favored the control-group test. A broader test that some courts employed extended the privilege to embrace any communication by an employee involving the employee's corporate duties and made at the direction of the employee's corporate employer. This latter test was favored by Chief Justice Burger in *Upjohn*, although the majority declined to formulate a standard. While avoiding some of the problems of the control group test, the broader test seems to unduly extend the shield of privilege.

Quicknotes

WORK-PRODUCT RULE A doctrine excluding from discovery work performed by an attorney in preparation of litigation.

In re Osterhoudt

Suspect in drug/tax violations (D) v. Federal government (P)

722 F.2d 591 (9th Cir. 1983)

NATURE OF CASE: Appeal from denial of motion to quash subpoena.

FACT SUMMARY: Defendant sought to quash a subpoena served on his attorney seeking information concerning defendant's legal fees. The trial court denied the motion and defendant appealed, contending that the records are protected by attorney-client privilege.

RULE OF LAW

The attorney-client privilege protects only confidential professional communications between the attorney and client and does not prohibit disclosure of non-privileged information such as a client's identity that might be used as evidence against the client.

FACTS: The federal Government (P) was investigating the defendant for possible marijuana sales and income tax violations, and the defendant hired William L. Osterhoudt, an attorney, for representation. As part of the investigation, the Government (P) subpoenaed Osterhoudt's records of defendant's legal fees. The defendant moved to quash, but the trial court denied the motion. The defendant appealed, claiming the records are protected by attorney-client privilege.

ISSUE: Does the attorney-client privilege protect only confidential professional communications between the attorney and client, and does it not prohibit disclosure of non-privileged information such as a client's identity that might be used as evidence against the client?

HOLDING AND DECISION: (Per curiam) Yes. The attorney-client privilege protects only confidential professional communications between the attorney and client and does not prohibit disclosure of non-privileged information such as a client's identity that might be used as evidence against the client. The defendant mischaracterizes the law when he argues that privilege attaches whenever the information sought would implicate the client in the matter for which he sought the attorney's guidance in the first place. The rule is that information preceding the attorney-client relationship, such as the client's name, and information that is not a professional communication, such as legal fees paid, are not protected by privilege. Cases that do grant privilege to such disclosures are misstating the holding of *Baird v. Koerner*, 270 F.2d 623 (9th Cir. 1960). *Baird* protected a client's identity through privilege because the identity was material only as an acknowledgment of guilt. In this case, the defendant's retention of and payment for Osterhoudt's services are not acknowledgment of his guilt. The Government (P) does not seek the content of a confidential professional communication, but merely the amounts and dates of defendant's payment of fees. Defendant also argues that compelling disclosure of this information will threaten attorney-client relationships. Confidentiality of legal fees could not have been seriously contemplated by defendant, so no true threat exists. Affirmed.

ANALYSIS

Attorneys should be circumspect about the disclosure of any client information, but privilege cannot protect every word out of the client's mouth or the mere fact of the client's existence. Attorneys should inform clients that discretion is a given, but that certain disclosures are simply not protected.

Quicknotes

ATTORNEY-CLIENT PRIVILEGE A doctrine precluding the admission into evidence of confidential communications between an attorney and the client made in the course of obtaining professional assistance.

United States v. Albertelli

Federal government (P) v. Individual convicted of, *inter alia*, extortion (D)

687 F.3d 439 (1st Cir.), *cert. denied*, 568 U.S. 994 (2012)

NATURE OF CASE: Appeal from conviction, *inter alia*, of extortion.

FACT SUMMARY: Albertelli (D) and others (D), who were convicted, *inter alia*, of extortion based on the attempted burning down of a competitors' building, contended that incriminating testimony provided by O'Connor, an attorney and Albertelli's (D) long-time friend, should have been excluded on the basis of the attorney-client privilege. The Government (P) contended that the crime-fraud exception to the privilege applied, so that it was proper to admit O'Connor's testimony.

RULE OF LAW

The attorney-client privilege is forfeited under the crime-fraud exception to the privilege, which excludes communications from a client to an attorney made (1) when the client was engaged in (or was planning) criminal or fraudulent activity, and (2) with the intent to facilitate or conceal the criminal or fraudulent activity.

FACTS: Albertelli (D) and others (D) were engaged in various criminal activities that were related to illegal gambling businesses. They were convicted of racketeering, racketeering conspiracy or both, and a host of other federal crimes related to the illegal gambling operations, including extortion based on the attempted burning down of a competitors' building that contained a restaurant. The Government (P) asserted that Albertelli's (D) and the others' (D) motive was extortion, by cutting off the competitors' income from the restaurant, whereas Albertelli (D) and the others (D) claimed that their motive was revenge. To support its case, the Government (P) called O'Connor, an attorney and Albertelli's (D) long-time friend, who testified over objection based on the attorney-client privilege, about a conversation he had with Albertelli (D) about "various strategies that might be employed to get control" of the restaurant from the "guys on the other side." According to O'Connor, "[Albertelli said] [i]f they could cut off their funds, wouldn't they then fall faster in a financial house of cards? And I said, Sure, but how is that going to happen? And Mr. Albertelli said, Well, . . .— what if there was a fire at the [restaurant] and they weren't able to take any income out of the place?" As O'Connor vehemently discouraged such an effort, Albertelli (D) inquired, "[H]ow illegal is arson?" The district court permitted O'Connor's testimony, and the First Circuit Court of Appeals granted review.

ISSUE: Is the attorney-client privilege forfeited under the crime-fraud exception to the privilege, which excludes communications from a client to an attorney made (1) when the client was engaged in (or was planning) criminal or fraudulent activity, and (2) with the intent to facilitate or conceal the criminal or fraudulent activity?

HOLDING AND DECISION: (Boudin, J.) Yes. The attorney-client privilege is forfeited under the crime-fraud exception to the privilege, which excludes communications from a client to an attorney made (1) when the client was engaged in (or was planning) criminal or fraudulent activity, and (2) with the intent to facilitate or conceal the criminal or fraudulent activity. Whether or not O'Connor was acting as Albertelli's (D) lawyer in the conversation or merely as a friend, Albertelli (D) forfeited the privilege under the crime-fraud exception. Although in some circumstances nothing sinister is implied by asking an attorney about the legality of conduct, possible penalties or both, here Albertelli (D) certainly knew that arson was illegal, and his threshold question—"If they could cut off their funds . . . "— revealed his motive for the crime and the intent to facilitate its commission through his inquiries of O'Connor. Once a plan to commit a crime is conceived, disclosing that to an attorney waives the privilege. Affirmed as to this issue.

ANALYSIS

The attorney-client privilege is a well-established historic rule that protects confidential communications between client and attorney. The privilege belongs to the client, not the attorney. The United States Supreme Court has long emphasized that the central concern of the privilege is to encourage full and frank communication between attorneys and their clients and thereby promote broader public interests in the observance of law and administration of justice. See, *United States v. Zolin*, 491 U.S. 554 (1989). This privilege under federal law is the oldest of the privileges for confidential communications known to the common law. However, the privilege is not lost through the crime-fraud exception if a client proposes a course of conduct that the client is advised by counsel is illegal, but, as is illustrated by *Albertelli*, is extinguished when a client seeks legal advice to further a continuing or future crime. Because this ancient and valuable attorney-client privilege is at

Continued on next page.

the expense of the full discovery of the truth, it should be strictly construed.

Quicknotes

ATTORNEY-CLIENT PRIVILEGE A doctrine precluding the admission into evidence of confidential communications between an attorney and the client made in the course of obtaining professional assistance.

EXTORTION The unlawful taking of property of another by threats of force.

INTER ALIA Among other things.

Jaffee v. Redmond

Executor of estate (P) v. Police officer (D)

518 U.S. 1 (1996)

NATURE OF CASE: Appeal from an award of damages in a wrongful-death action.

FACT SUMMARY: Redmond (D), a police officer, underwent counseling sessions after shooting a man and sought to keep those sessions confidential in the subsequent federal civil action brought by the man's estate (P).

RULE OF LAW

Confidential communications between a psychotherapist and his or her patient in the course of diagnosis and treatment are protected from compelled disclosure under Rule 501 of the Federal Rules of Evidence.

FACTS: Redmond (D), a police officer, shot and killed Allen while on duty. Jaffee (P), the executor of Allen's estate, filed a wrongful-death action against Redmond (D). Following the shooting, Redmond (D) had participated in 50 counseling sessions with Beyer, a clinical social worker. Jaffee (P) sought access to Beyer's notes for use at trial. Redmond (D) asserted that the counseling sessions were confidential and privileged. The district court disagreed, but Redmond (D) and Beyer refused to comply with the discovery order to disclose the notes. At the end of the trial, the court informed the jury that the refusal to turn over the notes was not justified and that the jury should presume that the contents were unfavorable to Redmond (D). The jury awarded $545,000 in damages to Jaffee (P), but Redmond (D) appealed and prevailed. Jaffee (P) appealed the reversal of the award.

ISSUE: Are confidential communications between a psychotherapist and his or her patient protected from compelled disclosure?

HOLDING AND DECISION: (Stevens, J.) Yes. Confidential communications between a psychotherapist and his or her patients in the course of diagnosis and treatment are protected from compelled disclosure under Rule 501 of the Federal Rules of Evidence. Rule 501 of the Federal Rules of Evidence authorizes federal courts to define new privileges by interpreting common-law principles in the light of reason and experience. Thus, it was recognized that the recognition of privileges would change over time. The recognition of a privilege based on a confidential relationship should be determined on a case-by-case basis, taking into account the public good that would result from allowing the privilege. Of course, privileges should still be rare because they are an exception to the general rule favoring access to all probative evidence. The psychotherapist–patient privilege is rooted in the imperative need for confidence and trust. Successful treatment for mental illnesses depends on complete openness between the psychotherapist and the patient. The mental health of the public depends in part on the confidentiality between patients and psychotherapists. In contrast, the evidentiary benefit from denying the privilege would be modest. Patients would be chilled from expression in situations where litigation was imminent. The privilege should be extended to all licensed social workers who perform mental health treatment. Accordingly, the communications between Redmond (D) and Beyer were privileged, and the trial court should not have directed the jury to make a negative inference from the refusal to divulge the contents of Beyer's notes. Affirmed.

DISSENT: (Scalia, J.) While the majority goes to great lengths to show the benefit that will result from this privilege, they give short shrift to the loss of probative evidence that will cause injustice in many cases. Furthermore, the majority does not make it clear why the privilege should extend to social workers when the privilege has usually been limited to those who actually practice medicine.

ANALYSIS

Prior to this decision, the court of appeals had split on this issue. Most states recognize this privilege, although most of these states extend the privilege through statute rather than common-law principles. Justice Scalia also pointed out in dissent that it was not realistic to suggest that people would fail to seek therapy because the therapist might have to turn over notes by court order.

Quicknotes

FED. R. EVID. 501 Provides that privilege principles shall be based on common law.

PSYCHOTHERAPIST–PATIENT PRIVILEGE The right of a patient to refuse to reveal confidential information given during the course of a relationship with a physician entered into for the purpose of treatment.

Trammel v. United States

Indicted drug dealer (D) v. Federal government (P)

445 U.S. 40 (1980)

NATURE OF CASE: Appeal from convictions for conspiracy to import and importing heroin.

FACT SUMMARY: Trammel's (D) wife agreed to testify against her husband in return for lenient treatment for herself, but Trammel (D) argued he had the right to prevent her from testifying against him.

RULE OF LAW

A criminal defendant cannot prevent his or her spouse from voluntarily giving testimony against him or her because the privilege against adverse spousal testimony belongs to the testifying spouse.

FACTS: In return for lenient treatment for herself, Mrs. Trammel, an unindicted co-conspirator, agreed to testify against her husband at his trial for conspiracy to import and importing heroin. The district court ruled she could testify to any act she observed during the marriage and to any communication made in the presence of a third person but not as to confidential communications between herself and her husband because they fell within the privilege attaching to confidential marital communications. On appeal, Trammel (D) contended that he was entitled to invoke the privilege against adverse spousal testimony so as to exclude the voluntary testimony of his wife. The court of appeals rejected this contention and affirmed the convictions.

ISSUE: Can a criminal defendant invoke the privilege against adverse spousal testimony so as to prevent his or her spouse from voluntarily offering adverse testimony against him or her?

HOLDING AND DECISION: (Burger, C.J.) No. Inasmuch as the privilege against adverse spousal testimony belongs solely to the testifying spouse, a criminal defendant cannot invoke the privilege to prevent his or her spouse from offering adverse testimony against him or her. The *Hawkins v. United States*, 358 U.S. 74 (1958), case left the federal privilege for adverse spousal testimony where it found it at the time, thus continuing a rule that barred the testimony of one spouse against the other unless both consented. However, since that 1958 decision, support for that conception of the privilege has eroded further and the trend in state law is toward divesting the accused of the privilege to bar adverse spousal testimony. The ancient foundations for so sweeping a privilege involved a conception of the wife as her husband's chattel to do with as he wished, and they have long since disappeared. Nor is the desire to protect the marriage a valid justification for affording an accused such a privilege. If his spouse desires to testify against him, simply preventing her from doing so is not likely to save the marriage. Affirmed.

ANALYSIS

The Model Code of Evidence and the Uniform Rules of Evidence completely abolished the notion of a privilege against adverse spousal testimony and limited themselves to recognizing a privilege covering confidential marital communications. Several state legislatures have followed suit.

United States v. Montgomery

Federal government (P) v. Alleged conspirator (D)

384 F.3d 1050 (9th Cir. 2004)

NATURE OF CASE: Appeal from convictions for conspiracy and mail fraud.

FACT SUMMARY: A wife testified against her husband at his criminal trial, and an incriminating letter she wrote to him was also admitted into evidence against him.

RULE OF LAW

Either spouse can invoke the "marital communications" privilege to exclude communications made between spouses while they were married.

FACTS: Montgomery (D) and his sister formed a company that rented out owners' vacation homes in exchange for commissions of 25 to 30 percent. Montgomery's (D) wife, Louise, eventually suspected his sister of diverting funds from the homeowners by renting the properties and failing to inform the owners of the rentals. Louise discussed her suspicions with Montgomery (D) and later expressed her concerns in a letter to him; she left the letter for him on the kitchen counter in their home, and she intended for him to convey the letter's contents to his sister. After these communications, Louise joined the conspiracy with Montgomery (D) and his sister and participated in the scheme of diverting funds from the homeowners. At Montgomery's (D) trial for conspiracy and mail fraud, Louise testified about her communications with Montgomery (D); the Government (P) also introduced the letter she wrote to Montgomery (D). Montgomery (D) was convicted, and he appealed.

ISSUE: Can either spouse invoke the "marital communications" privilege to exclude communications made between spouses while they were married?

HOLDING AND DECISION: (Goodwin, J.) Yes. Either spouse can invoke the "marital communications" privilege to exclude communications made between spouses while they were married. Federal courts recognize two evidentiary privileges grounded in the marital relationship. The first belongs solely to the witness spouse, who thus may waive the privilege as Louise did here. The second privilege is known as the "marital communications" privilege. It excludes (1) words and acts those spouses intended as communications (2) if there is a valid marriage and (3) if the communications were confidential. The burden is on the Government (P) to show that spouses did not intend for a communication to be confidential. Here, the sole issue is whether Louise intended for her letter to remain confidential. Marital communications are presumptively confidential, but the presumption is rebutted where a third party is present or where the communication was intended for transmittal to a third person. The Government (P) has failed to rebut the presumption of confidentiality for Louise's letter because her desire that Montgomery (D) would communicate her concerns to his sister is insufficient and because there is no evidence that the couple's children could have seen the letter. Furthermore, the clear majority of jurisdictions hold that either spouse can invoke the "marital communications" privilege, and Montgomery (D) thus can invoke the privilege here. The trial court therefore erred by admitting Louise's letter and permitting the Government (P) to question her about her communications with Montgomery (D). Moreover, the Government (P) also has failed to show that an exception justified the otherwise-erroneous admission of Louise's communications. First, the record demonstrates no completed crime for which Louise could have been an accessory after the fact, and the Court therefore need not reach the question of whether the "accessory after the fact" exception defeats the privilege. Second, the "partnership in crime" exception does not apply because, under the Government's (P) own theory of the case, at the time of the communications Louise had not yet joined forces with Montgomery (D) and his sister. Reversed.

ANALYSIS

The distinction between marital privileges illustrated by *Montgomery* is fine but profound. One privilege belongs exclusively to the communicating spouse; as this case shows, that spouse can waive this narrow first privilege and testify if she so desires. The broader second privilege, however, may be invoked by either spouse. It is not universally accepted, though, and one should consult local law to ensure whether, and under what conditions, the broader "marital communications" privilege might be available in a particular jurisdiction.

Quicknotes

MARITAL PRIVILEGE Privilege for communications made between spouses during their marriage, which may be exercised at the option of the witness spouse, rendering the communication inadmissible.

CHAPTER 13

Foundational Evidence, Authentication

Quick Reference Rules of Law

United States v. Johnson

Federal government (P) v. Convicted felon (D)

637 F.2d 1224 (9th Cir. 1980)

NATURE OF CASE: Appeal from an assault conviction.

FACT SUMMARY: Johnson (D) contended the trial court erred in admitting into evidence an ax that was not properly authenticated by the prosecution.

RULE OF LAW

Federal Rule of Evidence 901 provides that the requirement of authentication as a condition precedent to admissibility is satisfied by evidence sufficient to support a finding that the matter in question is what its proponent claims.

FACTS: Johnson (D) was arrested for an attack with an ax on a victim named Papse. At trial, the prosecution called Papse as a witness and attempted to authenticate an ax as the weapon of assault. Papse identified the ax; however, he could not distinguish that ax from any other ax and could not identify specific characteristics of this ax that could tie it to the incident. Johnson (D) contended this was insufficient authentication to allow the ax into evidence. The trial court allowed the ax into evidence, and Johnson (D) was convicted. He appealed, contending the trial court erred in admitting the ax.

ISSUE: Is the requirement of authentication as a condition precedent to admissibility satisfied by evidence sufficient to support a finding that the matter in question is what its proponent claims?

HOLDING AND DECISION: (Williams, J.) Yes. Federal Rule of Evidence 901 provides that the requirement of authentication as a condition precedent to admissibility is satisfied by evidence sufficient to support a finding that the matter in question is what its proponent claims. In this case, the prosecution merely had to provide sufficient evidence that the ax produced in court was the ax used in the incident. It was not required to establish that the witness could distinguish this ax from any other ax, nor was it required to have the witness testify as to the specific characteristics of this ax. While the identification may not have been entirely free from doubt, the witness did state that he was pretty sure this was the weapon that had been used against him. He further testified that he was personally familiar with the particular ax because he had used it in the past. Thus, a reasonable juror could have found that this ax was the weapon allegedly used in the assault. Thus, there was no abuse of discretion in the trial court's ruling that proper authentication was made. As a result, the conviction must stand.

ANALYSIS

This case illustrates that in federal court, as well as in most state courts, the initial condition precedent to allowing materials into evidence is proper authentication. The requirement is that the proponent of the evidence present sufficient evidence that the particular material is what it purports to be. When dealing with documentary evidence, a witness familiar with either the preparation of the document, or familiar with the handwriting of the person creating the document is usually sufficient for that witness to testify that the particular documentary evidence is what it purports to be. Authentication does not establish the weight to be given to the particular piece of evidence; it merely allows the material into evidence so that the trier of fact can then weigh its reliability against any countervailing evidence. Usually when dealing with evidence of either a documentary or other nature, the chain of custody of the evidence is an important issue to be established by the proponent. A failure to account for the chain of possession of evidence from the incident involved to the trial may lead to its exclusion.

Quicknotes

AUTHENTICATION (OF DOCUMENTARY EVIDENCE) The validity of documentary evidence that must be established prior to its admission into evidence, usually by showing that a document is what it purports to be.

FED. R. EVID. 901 Sets forth the means of compliance with the requirement of authentication as a condition precedent to admissibility.

United States v. Howard-Arias

Federal government (P) v. Convicted drug dealer (D)

679 F.2d 363 (4th Cir. 1982)

NATURE OF CASE: Appeal of conviction for drug-related offenses.

FACT SUMMARY: Howard-Arias (D) contended that seized contraband could not be introduced into evidence because one of the individuals involved in the "chain of custody" did not testify.

RULE OF LAW

Tangible evidence will not be made inadmissible merely because one custodian thereof fails to testify.

FACTS: A large amount of marijuana was found on a disabled ship on which Howard-Arias (D) had been a crew member. The U.S. Coast Guard took both Howard-Arias (D) and the marijuana into custody. Howard-Arias (D) objected, as one of the persons forming the "chain of custody" did not testify regarding authentication. The district court overruled the objection, and Howard-Arias (D) was convicted. He appealed.

ISSUE: Will tangible evidence be made inadmissible merely because one custodian thereof fails to testify?

HOLDING AND DECISION: [Judge not stated in casebook excerpt.] No. Tangible evidence will not be made inadmissible merely because one custodian thereof fails to testify. Real evidence must be authenticated prior to admission. This is to ensure that the proffered item is in fact that which it is purported to be. The question is whether the authentication testimony is sufficiently complete so as to convince the court that the original item was, in fact, what was offered. This is a matter for the trial court's discretion; there is no rule that every custodian of the item needs to testify. Here, it is well within the court's discretion to find contraband authenticated. Affirmed.

ANALYSIS

Not all courts have been as lenient with authentication as this one. Many courts have rejected evidence due to a failure to produce each custodian thereof. Because of the reasonable doubt standard in criminal cases, the issue arises most often in criminal cases.

Quicknotes

AUTHENTICATION (OF DOCUMENTARY EVIDENCE) The validity of documentary evidence that must be established prior to its admission into evidence, usually by showing that a document is what it purports to be.

United States v. Bagaric

Federal government (P) v. Convicted felon (D)

706 F.2d 42 (2d Cir. 1983)

NATURE OF CASE: Appeal under the Racketeer Influenced and Corrupt Organizations Act.

FACT SUMMARY: A letter incriminating as to Logarusic (D) was deemed authentic because it was replete with references to Logarusic's (D) circle of conspirators.

RULE OF LAW

A letter may be authenticated by the names contained therein.

FACTS: Logarusic (D), Bagaric (D), Markich (D), Primorac (D), Sudar (D), and Ljubas (D) were indicted under the Racketeer Influenced and Corrupt Organizations Act. At trial, the Government (P) sought to introduce a letter found during a search of Logarusic's (D) home. The letter contained incriminating information. It was addressed to Logarusic (D) from Bagaric (D) and contained numerous references to the circle of indicted conspirators, including aliases. Over Logarusic's (D) foundational objection, the letter was admitted into evidence. Logarusic (D) was convicted, and he appealed, arguing that the letter could not be authenticated by the names that appeared in it.

ISSUE: May a letter be authenticated by the names contained therein?

HOLDING AND DECISION: (Kaufman, J.) Yes. A letter may be authenticated by the names contained therein. The requirement of authentication, per Fed. R. Evid. 901(a), is satisfied by evidence sufficient to support a finding that the matter is what the proponent claims it is. Where the evidence at issue is a letter, the names contained therein can be sufficient to demonstrate this. Here, the names in the letter of the various defendants give ample support to the contention that the letter was in fact a correspondence from Bagaric (D) to Logarusic (D). Affirmed.

ANALYSIS

The requirement of authentication was rather strict at common law. The proof that the connection between proffered evidence and a party did, in fact, exist had to be convincing. Today, under Fed. R. Evid. 901(b), the evidence of authentication need only be sufficient to support an authentication finding.

Quicknotes

AUTHENTICATION (OF DOCUMENTARY EVIDENCE) The validity of documentary evidence that must be established prior to its admission into evidence, usually by showing that a document is what it purports to be.

RICO ACT The Racketeer Influenced and Corrupt Organization Act; federal and state statutes enacted for the purpose of prosecuting organized crime.

United States v. Oslund

Federal government (P) v. Individual (D)

453 F.3d 1048 (8th Cir. 2006)

NATURE OF CASE: Appeal from lower court's conviction of an individual for murder.

FACT SUMMARY: After Oslund (D) shot and killed a Brinks security guard outside of a Target store, the Federal Bureau of Investigation used an acquaintance of Oslund (D) to record conversations in which Oslund (D) explained to the acquaintance how he carried out the murder.

RULE OF LAW

Admission of tape-recorded conversations at trial is proper if the totality of the circumstances satisfies the court as to the recordings' reliability.

FACTS: Oslund (D) shot and killed a Brinks security guard during a robbery outside of a Target store. Following the murder, Federal Bureau of Investigation (FBI) agent James Walden approached an acquaintance of Oslund (D), Thomas Russell, who agreed to record conversations with Oslund (D) regarding the murder. While being recorded, Russell informed Oslund (D) that he wanted to carry out a similar robbery of a security guard. Oslund (D) discussed with Russell how he carried out the Target murder and robbery. Prior to trial, Oslund (D) moved to suppress the tape recordings. The court held an evidentiary hearing at which Russell and Agent Walden testified as to the recordings' creation. The court denied the motion. At the trial stage, the prosecution used only Agent Walden to authenticate the tapes because Russell was in jail at the time. After conviction, Oslund (D) appealed on the grounds the prosecution did not properly authenticate the tapes.

ISSUE: Is admission of tape-recorded conversations at trial proper if the totality of the circumstances satisfies the court as to the recordings' reliability?

HOLDING AND DECISION: (Hansen, J.) Yes. Admission of tape-recorded conversations at trial is proper if the totality of the circumstances satisfies the court as to the recordings' reliability. A list of several nonexclusive factors exist to determine the admissibility of recorded statements: (1) the recording device was capable of taping the conversation; (2) a competent person operated the device; (3) the recording is authentic; (4) there have been no modifications to the recording; (5) the recording has been properly preserved; (6) the speakers in the recording can be identified; and (7) the conversation recorded was made voluntarily, in good faith and without inducement. These are factors only and not a rigid set of elements that must all be satisfied. Oslund (D) first argues the tapes must be suppressed because Russell did not testify at trial. While it would have been better for him to testify, Agent Walden was competent to testify as to the creation of the recordings and the identity of the voices on the tape. In addition, while there are gaps in the recordings, their existence goes to the weight of the evidence and not the tapes' admissibility. Also, Oslund (D) argues Russell induced him to speak about the Target murder in order to collect a portion of the $115,000 reward money. However, Oslund (D) presented no evidence at trial that he was induced to speak about the murder. Because the totality of the circumstances satisfies the court as to the reliability of the tapes, their admission was not an abuse of discretion. Affirmed.

ANALYSIS

The best practice is always to call the person who made the tape recordings as a witness at trial. Here, the prosecution was able to use Agent Walden at trial, but the result may have been different if Russell had also not been available at the evidentiary hearing on Oslund's (D) motion to suppress. Once the trial court heard from Russell at the evidentiary stage, Oslund (D) faced a difficult hurdle to keep the tapes out of evidence.

Quicknotes

EVIDENTIARY HEARING Hearing pertaining to the evidence of the case.

United States v. Pool

Federal government (P) v. Convicted drug smuggler (D)

660 F.2d 547 (5th Cir. 1981)

NATURE OF CASE: Appeal of conviction for marijuana importation.

FACT SUMMARY: Loye (D) was convicted after a Government (P) agent who had never met Loye (D) received a telephone call in which an individual identifying himself as Loye (D) made incriminating statements.

RULE OF LAW

A statement made over the telephone may be excluded from evidence if the caller's identity cannot be established.

FACTS: While doing an undercover investigation of a drug smuggling operation, Drug Enforcement Administration agent Starratt received a telephone call from an individual identifying himself as "Chip," a nickname used throughout the investigation. Agent Starratt had never met Loye (D), nor theretofore heard his voice. Based partially on these statements, Loye (D) was indicted and convicted. He appealed.

ISSUE: May a statement made over the telephone be excluded from evidence if the caller's identity cannot be established?

HOLDING AND DECISION: (Hill, J.) Yes. A statement made over the telephone may be excluded from evidence if the caller's identity cannot be established. For a telephone call to be admitted into evidence, at least a prima facie case must be made regarding authentication of the caller's identity. No particular type of proof is determinative. However, a mere self-identification by the caller, unaccompanied by anything else, is not sufficient. Here, self-identification was all that was offered to authenticate, as Agent Starratt had no personal knowledge as to Loye's (D) voice characteristics. This was insufficient authentication. Reversed.

ANALYSIS

Numerous possible ways of authenticating a telephone call can be envisioned. Recording the caller's voice is a possibility. Another possibility would be the recipient of the call being familiar with the caller. Whether any of these would suffice in any given situation would depend on the facts of the case.

Quicknotes

AUTHENTICATION (OF DOCUMENTARY EVIDENCE) The validity of documentary evidence that must be established prior to its admission into evidence, usually by showing that a document is what it purports to be.

PRIMA FACIE CASE An action where the plaintiff introduces sufficient evidence to submit the issue to the judge or jury for determination.

CHAPTER 14

The "Best Evidence" Doctrine

Quick Reference Rules of Law

United States v. Duffy

Federal government (P) v. Convicted thief (D)

454 F.2d 809 (5th Cir. 1972)

NATURE OF CASE: Appeal from a conviction for transporting a stolen vehicle in interstate commerce.

FACT SUMMARY: Two witnesses testified that a shirt found in a suitcase in the car Duffy (D) was accused of stealing had the laundry mark "D-U-F." Duffy (D) objected to the testimony and claimed the Best Evidence Rule required that the Government (P) produce the shirt.

RULE OF LAW

The Best Evidence Rule covers only writings; it does not require admission of physical, non-writing objects that are the basis for witness testimony.

FACTS: A car that had been brought into the Florida body shop where Duffy (D) worked disappeared over the same weekend he did. Both were later found in California. Duffy (D) was convicted of transporting a motor vehicle in interstate commerce knowing it to have been stolen. On appeal, he complained of error in the admission of certain evidence. Specifically, two witnesses had testified that the trunk of the stolen car had contained two suitcases when found, and that in one of the suitcases was a white shirt with the laundry mark "D-U-F." Duffy (D) argued that the Best Evidence Rule required the Government (D) to produce the shirt itself, because the laundry mark made it proper to treat the shirt as a "writing."

ISSUE: Does the Best Evidence Rule cover only writings, such that it does not require the admission of physical, non-writing objects that are the basis for witness testimony?

HOLDING AND DECISION: (Wisdom, J.) Yes. The Best Evidence Rule (the Rule) covers only writings; it does not require admission of physical, non-writing objects that are the basis for witness testimony. According to Professor McCormick, the Rule, as it exists today, may be stated as follows: "[I]n proving the terms of a writing, where such terms are material, the original writing must be produced unless it is shown to be unavailable for some reason other than the serious fault of the proponent." McCormick, Evidence 409 (1954). When, as in this case, the disputed evidence is an object bearing a mark or inscription, and is, therefore, a chattel and a writing, the trial judge has discretion to treat the evidence as a chattel or as a writing. Here, the inscription on the shirt was simple and there was little danger that it could not be accurately remembered. Furthermore, its terms were by no means central or critical to the case, the shirt being only collateral evidence of the crime and only one piece of evidence in a substantial case against Duffy (D). Thus, the policy considerations behind the Rule are not present and the judge acted properly in treating the shirt as chattel instead of as a writing. Affirmed.

ANALYSIS

A number of courts agree with legal scholars Professors Wigmore and McCormick that the trial judge should have the discretion to decide whether the Best Evidence Rule should be applied in any individual case involving an inscribed chattel. However, the Uniform Rules of Evidence adopt the strident position that any object carrying an inscription should be treated as a "writing."

Quicknotes

BEST EVIDENCE RULE An evidentiary rule requiring that an original document be introduced if possible; secondary evidence is only admissible after proof that the original was lost or destroyed through no fault of the proponent.

CHATTEL An article of personal property, as distinguished from real property; a thing personal and moveable.

SECONDARY EVIDENCE Evidence that is not primary nor the actual thing or document itself, but which nonetheless may be admissible at trial under certain circumstances.

Meyers v. United States

Businessman (D) v. Federal government (P)

171 F.2d 800 (D.C. Cir. 1948)

NATURE OF CASE: Appeal from conviction for perjury.

FACT SUMMARY: Meyers (D) contended that the Government (P) violated the Best Evidence Rule by allowing testimony as to what was contained in a transcript.

RULE OF LAW

The Best Evidence Rule is limited to cases where the contents of a writing are to be proved.

FACTS: Lamarre testified before a committee of the United States Senate investigating fraud and corruption in the conduct of World War II that he, and not General Bennett Meyers (D), was the actual owner of Aviation Electric Corporation, which had held numerous lucrative contracts with the Army Air Force. Meyers (D) was a deputy chief procurement officer for the Army Air Force. Lamarre was indicted for perjury, and Meyers (D) was indicted for suborning the perjury of Lamarre. During the trial, William P. Rogers, the chief counsel to the senatorial committee, was permitted to testify as to what Lamarre had sworn to the subcommittee. Later in the trial, the Government (P) introduced into evidence a stenographic transcript of Lamarre's testimony at the Senate hearing. After being convicted of the charges, Meyers (D) appealed, arguing that the trial court violated the Best Evidence Rule by allowing Rogers to testify, when the transcript of Lamarre's testimony was actually the best evidence of what had been stated before the subcommittee.

ISSUE: Is the Best Evidence Rule limited to cases where the contents of a writing are to be proved?

HOLDING AND DECISION: (Miller, J.) Yes. The Best Evidence Rule is limited to cases where the contents of a writing are to be proved. Here, there was no attempt to prove the contents of a writing; the issue was what Lamarre had said, not what the transcript contained. The transcript made from shorthand notes of his testimony was evidence of what he had said, but it was not the only admissible evidence concerning it. Rogers's testimony was equally competent and admissible whether given before or after the transcript was received in evidence. Statements alleged to be perjurious may be proved by any person who heard them, as well as by a reporter who recorded them in shorthand. Affirmed.

DISSENT: (Prettyman, J.) The testimony given by Lamarre before the Senate Committee was presented to the jury at trial in so unfair and prejudicial a fashion as to constitute reversible error. Rogers did not purport to be absolute in his reproduction but merely recited his unrefreshed recollection, and his recollection on each of the alleged incidents of perjury bears a striking resemblance to the succinct summations in the indictment. It is obvious that what Rogers gave as substance was an essence of his own distillation and not an attempt to reproduce the whole of Lamarre's testimony.

ANALYSIS

The Federal Rules of Evidence state that "[a]n original writing, recording, or photograph is required in order to prove its content unless these rules or a federal statute provides otherwise." See Fed. R. Evid. 1002.

Quicknotes

BEST EVIDENCE RULE An evidentiary rule requiring that an original document be introduced if possible; secondary evidence is only admissible after proof that the original was lost or destroyed through no fault of the proponent.

FED. R. EVID. 1002 The Federal Rule of Evidence codifying the common-law Best Evidence Rule.

Sylvania Electric Products v. Flanagan

Electric company (D) v. Employee (P)

352 F.2d 1005 (1st Cir. 1965)

NATURE OF CASE: Appeal of award of damages for breach of contract.

FACT SUMMARY: Flanagan (P) was permitted to introduce a summary of certain material records rather than the records themselves, without showing the unavailability thereof.

RULE OF LAW

Where material records are not shown to be unavailable, the records rather than summaries thereof must be introduced.

FACTS: Flanagan (P) performed certain excavation work for Sylvania Electric Products (Sylvania) (D). At the end of the project, Sylvania (D) disputed the number of hours that Flanagan (P) had devoted to the project. The contract called for Flanagan (P) to be paid on an hourly basis. Flanagan (P) sued for breach of contract. At trial, Flanagan (P) introduced a summary he had made of certain records that purported to show the amount of time spent on the project. Sylvania (D) objected based on the Best Evidence Rule. When asked by the court where the originals were, Flanagan (P) replied he had some at home. He never produced the originals, but the summary was admitted anyway. The jury awarded Flanagan (P) over $25,000, and Sylvania (D) appealed.

ISSUE: Where material records are not shown to be unavailable, must the records rather than summaries thereof be introduced?

HOLDING AND DECISION: (McEntee, J.) Yes. Where material records are not shown to be unavailable, the records rather than summaries thereof must be introduced. It is well settled that the best evidence that is obtainable in the circumstances of the case must be adduced to prove any disputed fact. The more central the records are to the issue of the case, the more strictly this rule will be enforced. This has been interpreted to require originals when available. Here, the records that were not produced purported to prove the number of hours worked, which was the central issue of the case. No showing of unavailability was made. This was error on the part of the district court. Reversed and remanded.

ANALYSIS

The Best Evidence Rule often comes into play with the hearsay rule. Such records are often business related. The business record exception to the hearsay rule must often be invoked to permit the records required by the Best Evidence Rule.

Quicknotes

BEST EVIDENCE RULE An evidentiary rule requiring that an original document be introduced if possible; secondary evidence is admissible only after proof that the original was lost or destroyed through no fault of the proponent of the evidence.

BREACH OF CONTRACT Unlawful failure by a party to perform its obligations pursuant to contract.

Glossary

Common Latin Words and Phrases Encountered in the Law

A FORTIORI: Because one fact exists or has been proven, therefore a second fact that is related to the first fact must also exist.

A PRIORI: From the cause to the effect. A term of logic used to denote that when one generally accepted truth is shown to be a cause, another particular effect must necessarily follow.

AB INITIO: From the beginning; a condition that has existed throughout, as in a marriage that was void ab initio.

ACTUS REUS: The wrongful act; in criminal law, such action as is sufficient to trigger criminal liability.

AD VALOREM: According to value; an ad valorem tax is imposed upon an item located within the taxing jurisdiction calculated by the value of such item.

AMICUS CURIAE: Friend of the court. Its most common usage takes the form of an amicus curiae brief, filed by a person who is not a party to an action but is nonetheless allowed to offer an argument supporting his or her legal interests.

ARGUENDO: In arguing. A statement, possibly hypothetical, made for the purpose of argument.

BILL QUIA TIMET: A bill to quiet title (establish ownership) to real property.

BONA FIDE: True, honest, or genuine. May refer to a person's legal position based on good faith or lacking notice of fraud (such as a bona fide purchaser for value) or to the authenticity of a particular document (such as a bona fide last will and testament).

CAUSA MORTIS: With approaching death in mind. A gift causa mortis is a gift given by a party who feels certain that death is imminent.

CAVEAT EMPTOR: Let the buyer beware. This maxim is reflected in the rule of law that a buyer purchases at his or her own risk because it is the buyer's responsibility to examine, judge, test, and otherwise inspect what he or she is buying.

CERTIORARI: A writ of review. Petitions for review of a case by the United States Supreme Court are most often done by means of a writ of certiorari.

CONTRA: On the other hand. Opposite. Contrary to.

CORAM NOBIS: Before us; a writ of error directed to the court that originally rendered the judgment.

CORAM VOBIS: Before you; a writ of error directed by an appellate court to a lower court to correct a factual error.

CORPUS DELICTI: The body of the crime; the requisite elements of a crime amounting to objective proof that a crime has been committed.

CUM TESTAMENTO ANNEXO, ADMINISTRATOR (ADMINISTRATOR C.T.A.): With will annexed; an administrator c.t.a. settles an estate pursuant to a will in which he or she is not appointed.

DE BONIS NON, ADMINISTRATOR (ADMINISTRATOR D.B.N.): Of goods not administered; an administrator d.b.n. settles a partially settled estate.

DE FACTO: In fact; in reality; actually. Existing in fact but not officially approved or engendered.

DE JURE: By right; lawful. Describes a condition that is legitimate "as a matter of law," in contrast to the term "de facto," which connotes something existing in fact but not legally sanctioned or authorized. For example, de facto segregation refers to segregation brought about by housing patterns, etc., whereas de jure segregation refers to segregation created by law.

DE MINIMUS: Of minimal importance; insignificant; a trifle; not worth bothering about.

DE NOVO: Anew; a second time; afresh. A trial de novo is a new trial held at the appellate level as if the case originated there and the trial at a lower level had not taken place.

DICTA: Generally used as an abbreviated form of obiter dicta, a term describing those portions of a judicial opinion incidental or not necessary to resolution of the specific question before the court. Such nonessential statements and remarks are not considered to be binding precedent.

DUCES TECUM: Refers to a particular type of writ or subpoena requesting a party or organization to produce certain documents in their possession.

EN BANC: Full bench. Where a court sits with all justices present rather than the usual quorum.

EX PARTE: For one side or one party only. An ex parte proceeding is one undertaken for the benefit of only one party, without notice to, or an appearance by, an adverse party.

EX POST FACTO: After the fact. An ex post facto law is a law that retroactively changes the consequences of a prior act.

EX REL.: Abbreviated form of the term "ex relatione," meaning upon relation or information. When the state brings an action in which it has no interest against an individual at the instigation of one who has a private interest in the matter.

FORUM NON CONVENIENS: Inconvenient forum. Although a court may have jurisdiction over the case, the action should be tried in a more conveniently located court, one to which parties and witnesses may more easily travel, for example.

GUARDIAN AD LITEM: A guardian appointed by the court to represent a minor or incompetent person in a legal action.

HABEAS CORPUS: You have the body. The modern writ of habeas corpus is a writ directing that a person (body) being detained (such as a prisoner) be brought before the court so that the legality of his or her detention can be judicially ascertained.

IN CAMERA: In private, in chambers. When a hearing is held before a judge in his or her chambers or when all spectators are excluded from the courtroom.

IN FORMA PAUPERIS: In the manner of a pauper. A party who proceeds in forma pauperis because of his or her poverty is one who is allowed to bring suit without liability for costs.

INFRA: Below, under. A word referring the reader to a later part of a book. (The opposite of supra.)

IN LOCO PARENTIS: In the place of a parent.

IN PARI DELICTO: Equally wrong; a court of equity will not grant requested relief to an applicant who is in pari delicto, or as much at fault in the transactions giving rise to the controversy as is the opponent of the applicant.

IN PARI MATERIA: On like subject matter or upon the same matter. Statutes relating to the same person or things are said to be in pari materia. It is a general rule of statutory construction that such statutes should be construed together, i.e., looked at as if they together constituted one law.

IN PERSONAM: Against the person. Jurisdiction over the person of an individual.

IN RE: In the matter of. Used to designate a proceeding involving an estate or other property.

IN REM: Signifies an action against the res, or thing. An action in rem is basically one that is taken directly against property, as distinguished from an action in personam, i.e., against the person.

INTER ALIA: Among other things. Used to show that the whole of a statement, pleading, list, statute, etc., has not been set forth in its entirety.

INTER PARTES: Between the parties. May refer to contracts, conveyances, or other transactions having legal significance.

INTER VIVOS: Between the living. An inter vivos gift is a gift made by a living grantor, as distinguished from bequests contained in a will, which pass upon the death of the testator.

IPSO FACTO: By the mere fact itself.

JUS: Law or the entire body of law.

LEX LOCI: The law of the place; the notion that the rights of parties to a legal proceeding are governed by the law of the place where those rights arose.

MALUM IN SE: Evil or wrong in and of itself; inherently wrong. Describes an act that is wrong by its very nature, as opposed to one which would not be wrong but for the fact that there is a specific legal prohibition against it (malum prohibitum).

MALUM PROHIBITUM: Wrong because prohibited, but not inherently evil. Describes something that is wrong because it is expressly forbidden by law but that is not in and of itself evil, e.g., speeding.

MANDAMUS: We command. A writ directing an official to take a certain action.

MENS REA: A guilty mind; a criminal intent. A term used to signify the mental state that accompanies a crime or other prohibited act. Some crimes require only a general mens rea (general intent to do the prohibited act), but others, like assault with intent to murder, require the existence of a specific mens rea.

MODUS OPERANDI: Method of operating; generally refers to the manner or style of a criminal in committing crimes, admissible in appropriate cases as evidence of the identity of a defendant.

NEXUS: A connection to.

NISI PRIUS: A court of first impression. A nisi prius court is one where issues of fact are tried before a judge or jury.

N.O.V. (NON OBSTANTE VEREDICTO): Notwithstanding the verdict. A judgment n.o.v. is a judgment given in favor of one party despite the fact that a verdict was returned in favor of the other party, the justification being that the verdict either had no reasonable support in fact or was contrary to law.

NUNC PRO TUNC: Now for then. This phrase refers to actions that may be taken and will then have full retroactive effect.

PENDENTE LITE: Pending the suit; pending litigation underway.

PER CAPITA: By head; beneficiaries of an estate, if they take in equal shares, take per capita.

PER CURIAM: By the court; signifies an opinion ostensibly written "by the whole court" and with no identified author.

PER SE: By itself, in itself; inherently.

PER STIRPES: By representation. Used primarily in the law of wills to describe the method of distribution where a person, generally because of death, is unable to take that which is left to him or her by the will of another, and therefore his or her heirs divide such property between them rather than take under the will individually.

PRIMA FACIE: On its face, at first sight. A prima facie case is one that is sufficient on its face, meaning that the evidence supporting it is adequate to establish the case until contradicted or overcome by other evidence.

PRO TANTO: For so much; as far as it goes. Often used in eminent domain cases when a property owner receives partial payment for his or her land without prejudice to his or her right to bring suit for the full amount he or she claims the land to be worth.

QUANTUM MERUIT: As much as the party deserves. Refers to recovery based on the doctrine of unjust enrichment in those cases in which a party has rendered valuable services or furnished materials that were accepted and enjoyed by another under circumstances that would reasonably notify the recipient that the rendering party expected to be paid. In essence, the law implies a contract to pay the reasonable value of the services or materials furnished.

QUASI: Almost like; as if; nearly. Essentially used to signify that one subject or thing is almost analogous to another but that material differences between them do exist. For example, a quasi-criminal proceeding is one that is not strictly criminal but shares enough of the same characteristics to require some of the same safeguards (e.g., procedural due process must be followed in a parole hearing).

QUID PRO QUO: Something for something. In contract law, the consideration, something of value, passed between the parties to render the contract binding.

RES GESTAE: Things done. In evidence law, this principle justifies the admission of a statement that would otherwise be hearsay when it is made so closely to the event in question as to be said to be a part of it, or with such spontaneity as not to have the possibility of falsehood.

RES IPSA LOQUITUR: The thing speaks for itself. This doctrine gives rise to a rebuttable presumption of negligence when the instrumentality causing the injury was within the exclusive control of the defendant, and the injury was one that does not normally occur unless a person has been negligent.

RES JUDICATA: A matter adjudged. Doctrine that provides that once a court of competent jurisdiction has rendered a final judgment or decree on the merits, that judgment or decree is conclusive upon the parties to the case and prevents them from engaging in any other litigation on the points and issues determined therein.

RESPONDEAT SUPERIOR: Let the master reply. This doctrine holds the master liable for the wrongful acts of his or her servant (or the principal for his or her agent) in those cases in which the servant (or agent) was acting within the scope of his or her authority at the time of the injury.

STARE DECISIS: To stand by or adhere to that which has been decided. The common law doctrine of stare decisis attempts to give security and certainty to the law by following the policy that once a principle of law as applicable to a certain set of facts has been set forth in a decision, it forms a precedent that will subsequently be followed, even though a different decision might be made were it the first time the question had arisen. Of course, stare decisis is not an inviolable principle and is departed from in instances where there is good cause (e.g., considerations of public policy led the Supreme Court to disregard prior decisions sanctioning segregation).

SUPRA: Above. A word referring a reader to an earlier part of a book. (The opposite of infra.)

ULTRA VIRES: Beyond the power. This phrase is most commonly used to refer to actions taken by a corporation that are beyond the power or legal authority of the corporation.

Addendum of French Derivatives

CHATTEL: Tangible personal property.

CY PRES: Doctrine permitting courts to apply trust funds to purposes not expressed in the trust but necessary to carry out the settlor's intent.

IN PAIS: Not pursuant to legal proceedings.

PER AUTRE VIE: For another's life; during another's life. In property law, an estate may be granted that will terminate upon the death of someone other than the grantee.

PROFIT A PRENDRE: A license to remove minerals or other produce from land.

VOIR DIRE: Process of questioning jurors as to their predispositions about the case or parties to a proceeding in order to identify those jurors displaying bias or prejudice.